MARVEL
ULTIMATE
SPIDER-MAN
VS
THE SINISTER 6

MARVEL UNIVERSE ULTIMATE SPIDER-MAN VS. THE SINISTER SIX VOL. 1. Contains material originally published in magazine form as MARVEL UNIVERSE ULTIMATE SPIDER-MAN VS. THE SINISTER SIX #1-4. First printing 2017. ISBN# 978-1-302-90258-2. Published by MARVEL WORLDWIDE, INC., a subsidiary of MARVEL ENTERTAINMENT, LLC. OFFICE OF PUBLICATION: 135 West 50th Street, New York, NY 10020. Copyright © 2017 MARVEL No similarity between any of the names, characters, persons, and/or institutions in this magazine with those of any living or dead person or institution is intended, and any such similarity which may exist is purely coincidental. **Printed in the U.S.A.** ALAN FINE, President, Marvel Entertainment; DAN BUCKLEY, President, TV, Publishing & Brand Management; JOE QUESADA, Chief Creative Officer; TOM BREVOORT, SVP of Publishing; DAVID BOGART, SVP of Business Affairs & Operations, Publishing & Partnership; C.B. CEBULSKI, VP of Brand Management & Development, Asia; DAVID GABRIEL, SVP of Sales & Marketing, Publishing; JEFF YOUNGQUIST, VP of Production & Special Projects; DAN CARR, Executive Director of Publishing Technology; ALEX MORALES, Director of Publishing Operations; SUSAN CRESPI, Production Manager; STAN LEE, Chairman Emeritus. For information regarding advertising in Marvel Comics or on Marvel.com, please contact Vit DeBellis, Integrated Sales Manager, at vdebellis@marvel.com. For Marvel subscription inquiries, please call 888-511-5480. **Manufactured between 11/11/2016 and 12/19/2016 by SHERIDAN, CHELSEA, MI, USA.**

10 9 8 7 6 5 4 3 2 1

MARVEL
ULTIMATE
SPIDER-MAN
VS
THE SINISTER 6

BASED ON THE TV SERIES WRITTEN BY
KEVIN BURKE & CHRIS "DOC" WYATT AND JACOB SEMAHN

DIRECTED BY
YOUNG KI YOON, JAE WOO KIM AND ROY BURDINE

ANIMATION PRODUCED BY
MARVEL ANIMATION STUDIOS WITH **FILM ROMAN**

ADAPTED BY
JOE CARAMAGNA

SPECIAL THANKS TO
HANNAH MCDONALD & PRODUCT FACTORY

EDITORS
CHRISTINA HARRINGTON WITH MARK BASSO

SENIOR EDITOR
MARK PANICCIA

SPIDER-MAN CREATED BY **STAN LEE & STEVE DITKO**

Collection Editor: **Jennifer Grünwald**
Associate Managing Editor: **Kateri Woody**
Associate Editor: **Sarah Brunstad**
Editor, Special Projects: **Mark D. Beazley**
VP Production & Special Projects: **Jeff Youngquist**
SVP Print, Sales & Marketing: **David Gabriel**
Head of Marvel Television: **Jeph Loeb**

Editor In Chief: **Axel Alonso**
Chief Creative Officer: **Joe Quesada**
Publisher: **Dan Buckley**
Executive Producer: **Alan Fine**

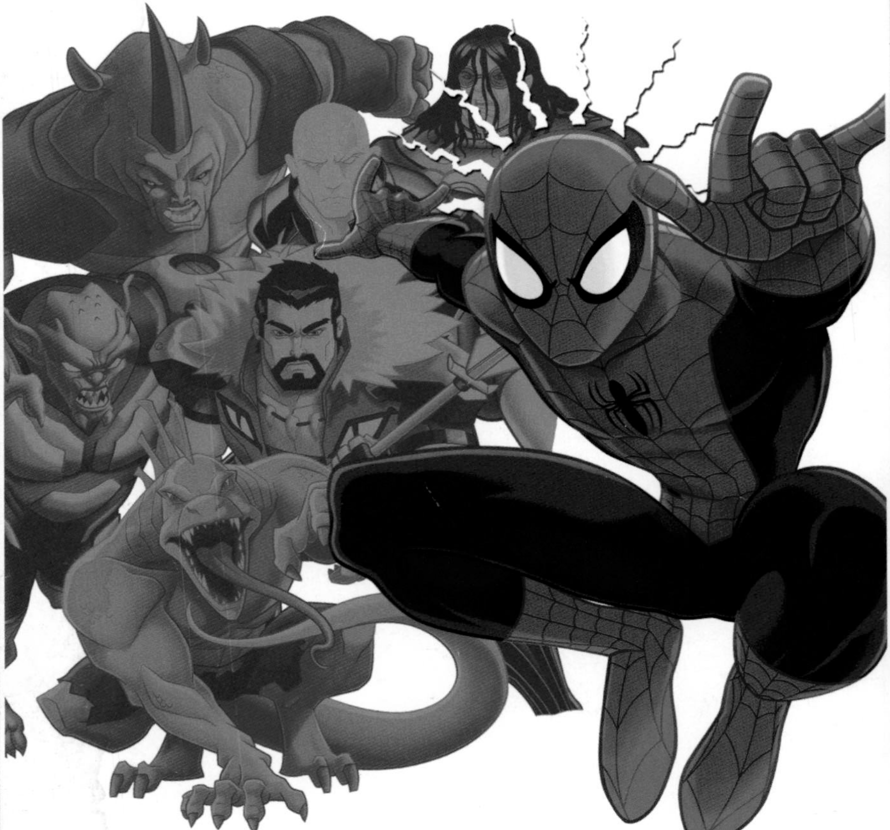

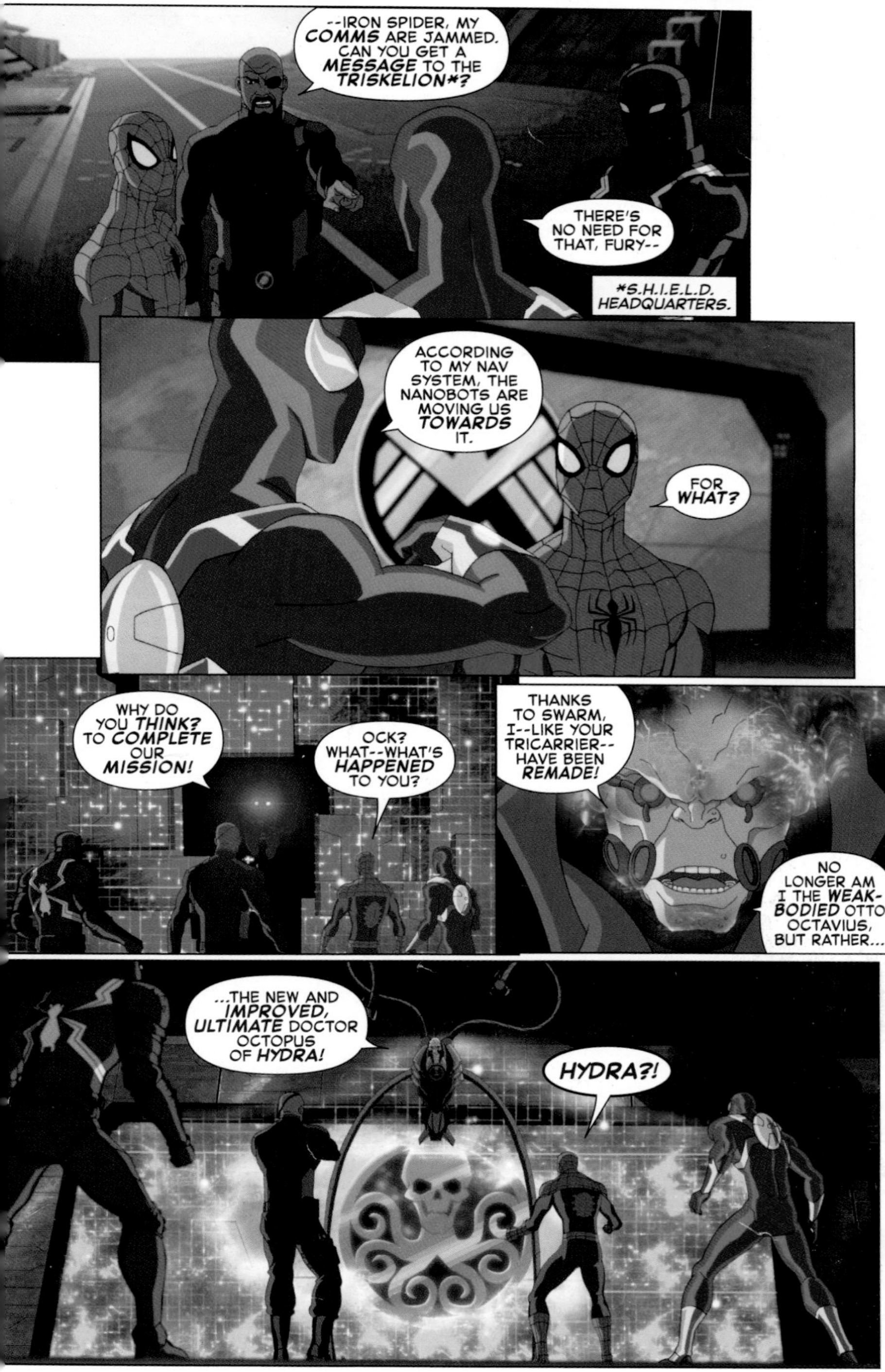
--IRON SPIDER, MY COMMS ARE JAMMED. CAN YOU GET A MESSAGE TO THE TRISKELION*?
THERE'S NO NEED FOR THAT, FURY--
*S.H.I.E.L.D. HEADQUARTERS.
ACCORDING TO MY NAV SYSTEM, THE NANOBOTS ARE MOVING US TOWARDS IT.
FOR WHAT?
WHY DO YOU THINK? TO COMPLETE OUR MISSION!
OCK? WHAT--WHAT'S HAPPENED TO YOU?
THANKS TO SWARM, I--LIKE YOUR TRICARRIER--HAVE BEEN REMADE!
NO LONGER AM I THE WEAK-BODIED OTTO OCTAVIUS, BUT RATHER...
...THE NEW AND IMPROVED, ULTIMATE DOCTOR OCTOPUS OF HYDRA!
HYDRA?!

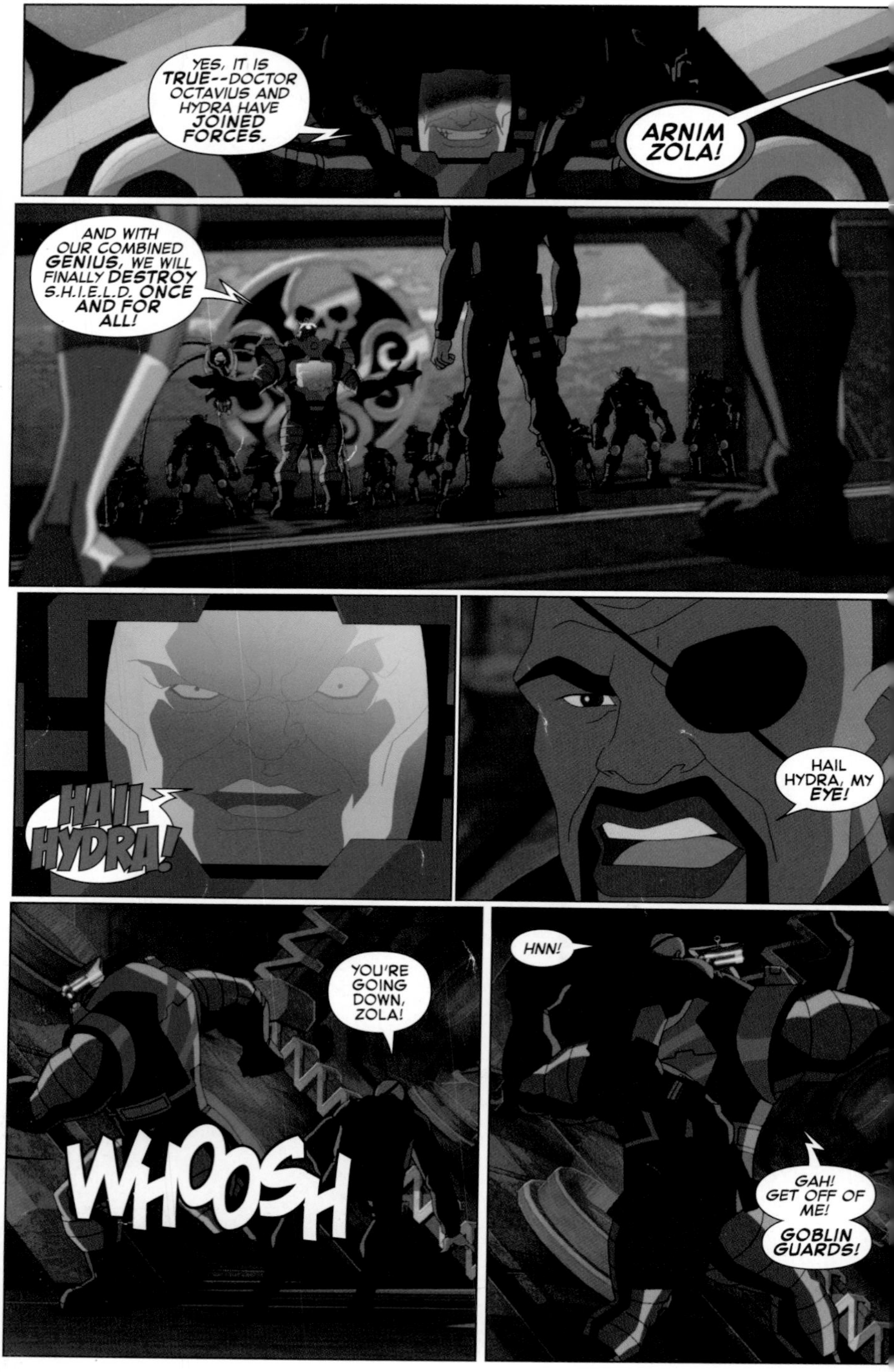
YES, IT IS TRUE--DOCTOR OCTAVIUS AND HYDRA HAVE JOINED FORCES.
ARNIM ZOLA!
AND WITH OUR COMBINED GENIUS, WE WILL FINALLY DESTROY S.H.I.E.L.D. ONCE AND FOR ALL!
HAIL HYDRA!
HAIL HYDRA, MY EYE!
YOU'RE GOING DOWN, ZOLA!
WHOOSH
HNN!
GAH! GET OFF OF ME!
GOBLIN GUARDS!

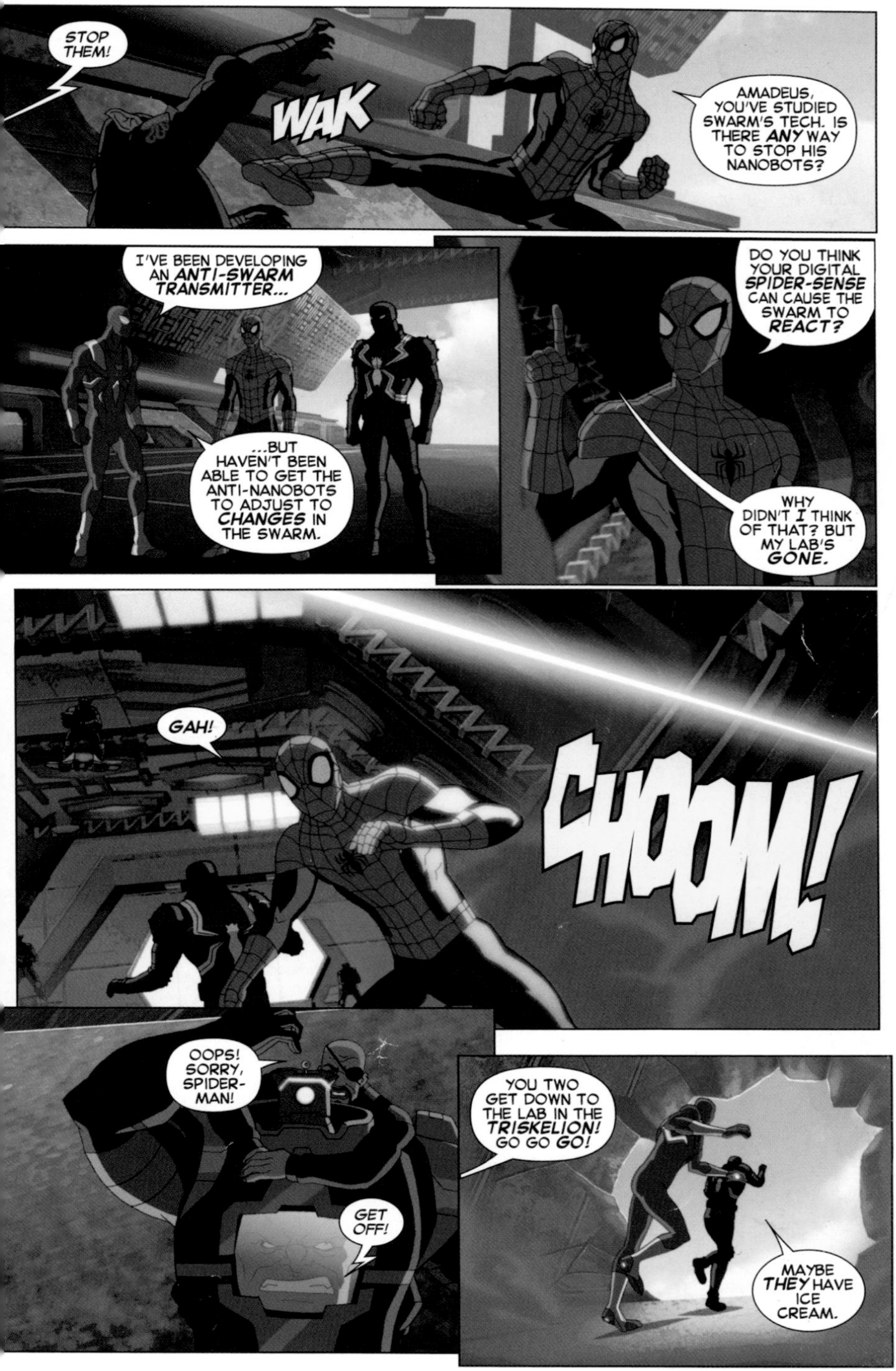
STOP THEM!
WAK
AMADEUS, YOU'VE STUDIED SWARM'S TECH. IS THERE ANY WAY TO STOP HIS NANOBOTS?
I'VE BEEN DEVELOPING AN ANTI-SWARM TRANSMITTER...
...BUT HAVEN'T BEEN ABLE TO GET THE ANTI-NANOBOTS TO ADJUST TO CHANGES IN THE SWARM.
DO YOU THINK YOUR DIGITAL SPIDER-SENSE CAN CAUSE THE SWARM TO REACT?
WHY DIDN'T I THINK OF THAT? BUT MY LAB'S GONE.
GAH!
CHOOM!
OOPS! SORRY, SPIDER-MAN!
GET OFF!
YOU TWO GET DOWN TO THE LAB IN THE TRISKELION! GO GO GO!
MAYBE THEY HAVE ICE CREAM.

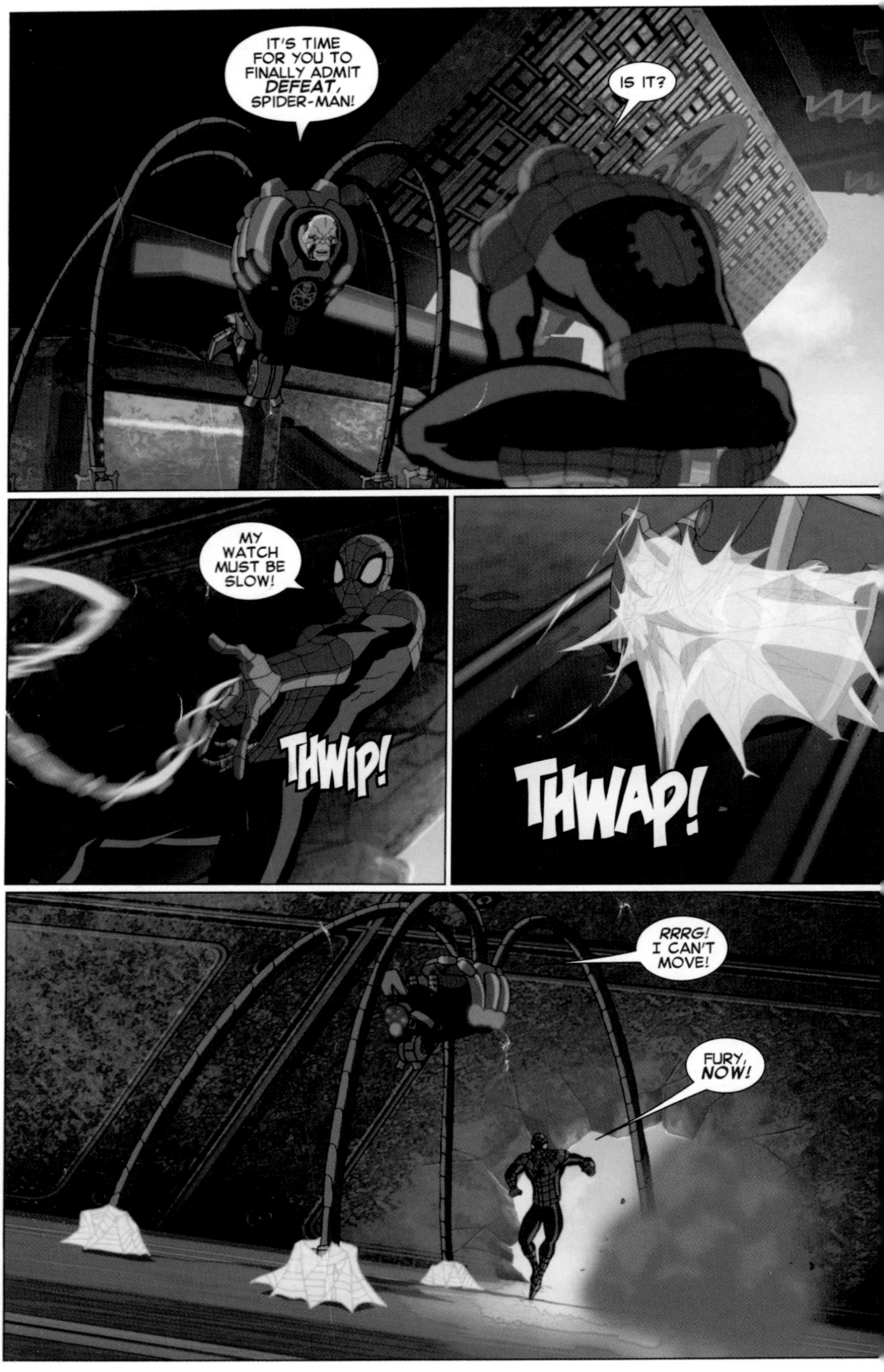

IT'S TIME FOR YOU TO FINALLY ADMIT *DEFEAT*, SPIDER-MAN!
IS IT?
MY WATCH MUST BE SLOW!
THWIP!
THWAP!
RRRG! I CAN'T MOVE!
FURY, **NOW!**

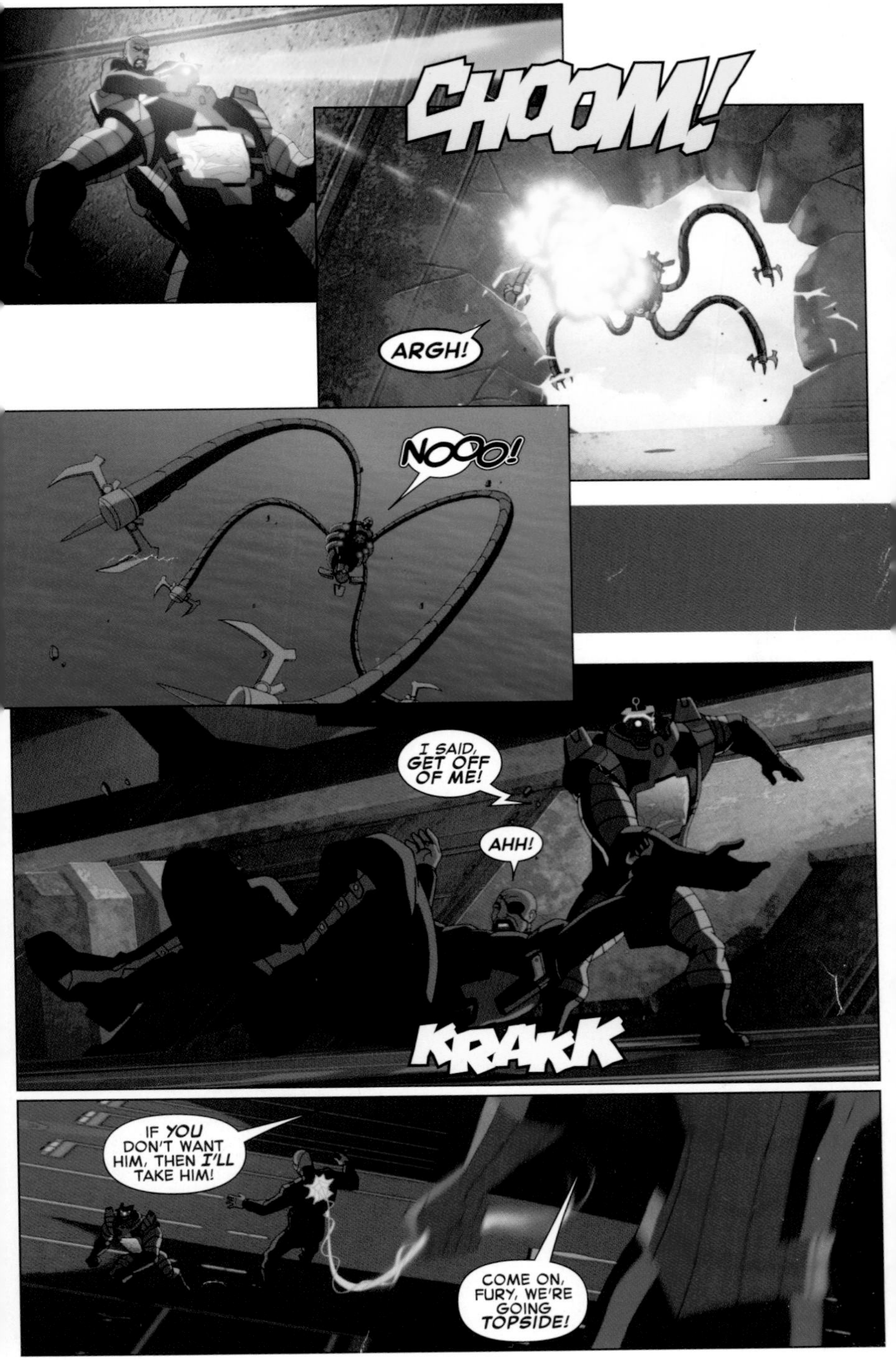
CHOOM!
ARGH!
NOOOO!
I SAID, GET OFF OF ME!
AHH!
KRAKK
IF YOU DON'T WANT HIM, THEN I'LL TAKE HIM!
COME ON, FURY, WE'RE GOING TOPSIDE!

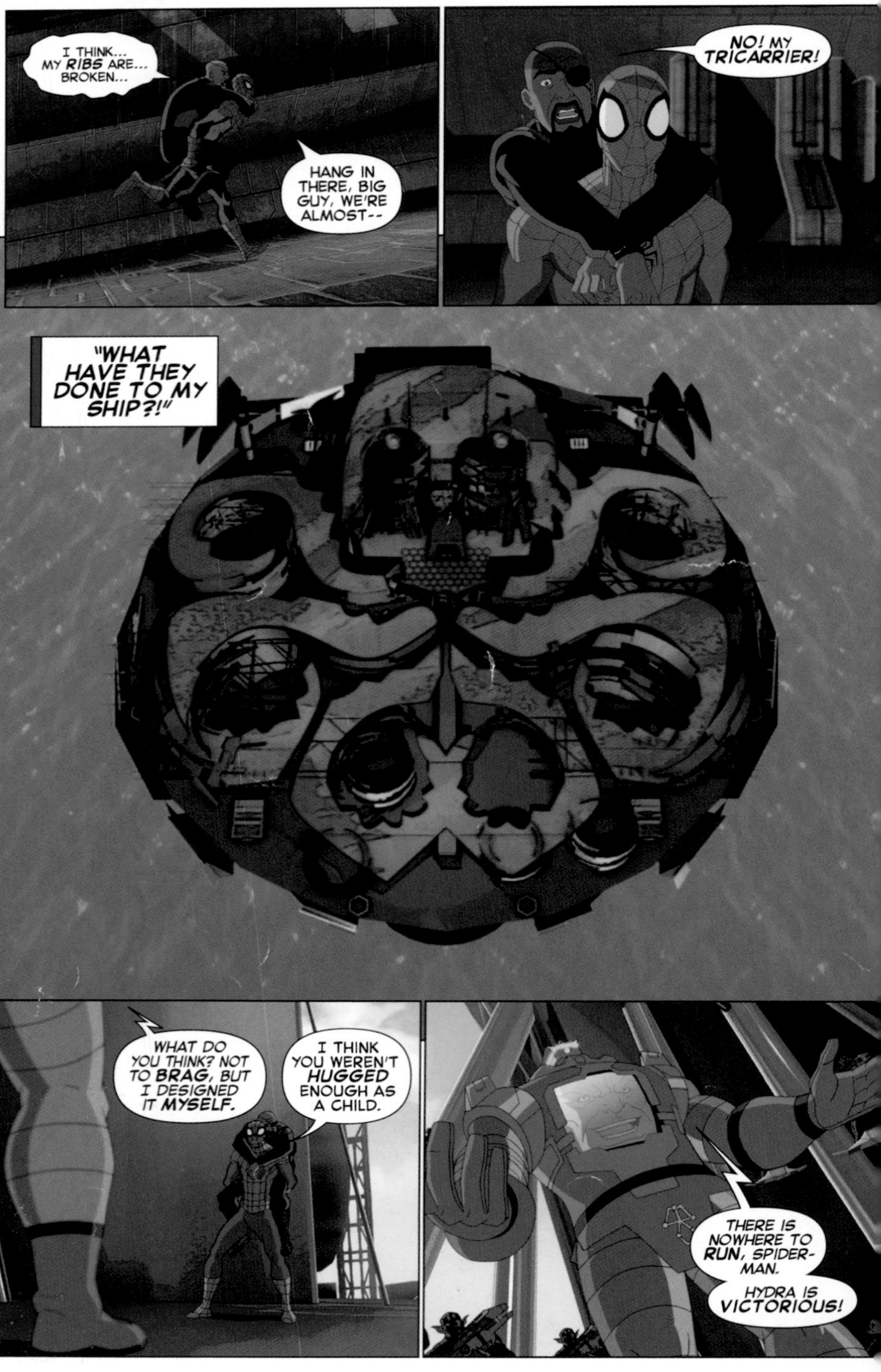
I THINK... MY RIBS ARE... BROKEN...
HANG IN THERE, BIG GUY, WE'RE ALMOST--
NO! MY TRICARRIER!
"WHAT HAVE THEY DONE TO MY SHIP?!"
WHAT DO YOU THINK? NOT TO BRAG, BUT I DESIGNED IT MYSELF.
I THINK YOU WEREN'T HUGGED ENOUGH AS A CHILD.
THERE IS NOWHERE TO RUN, SPIDER-MAN.
HYDRA IS VICTORIOUS!

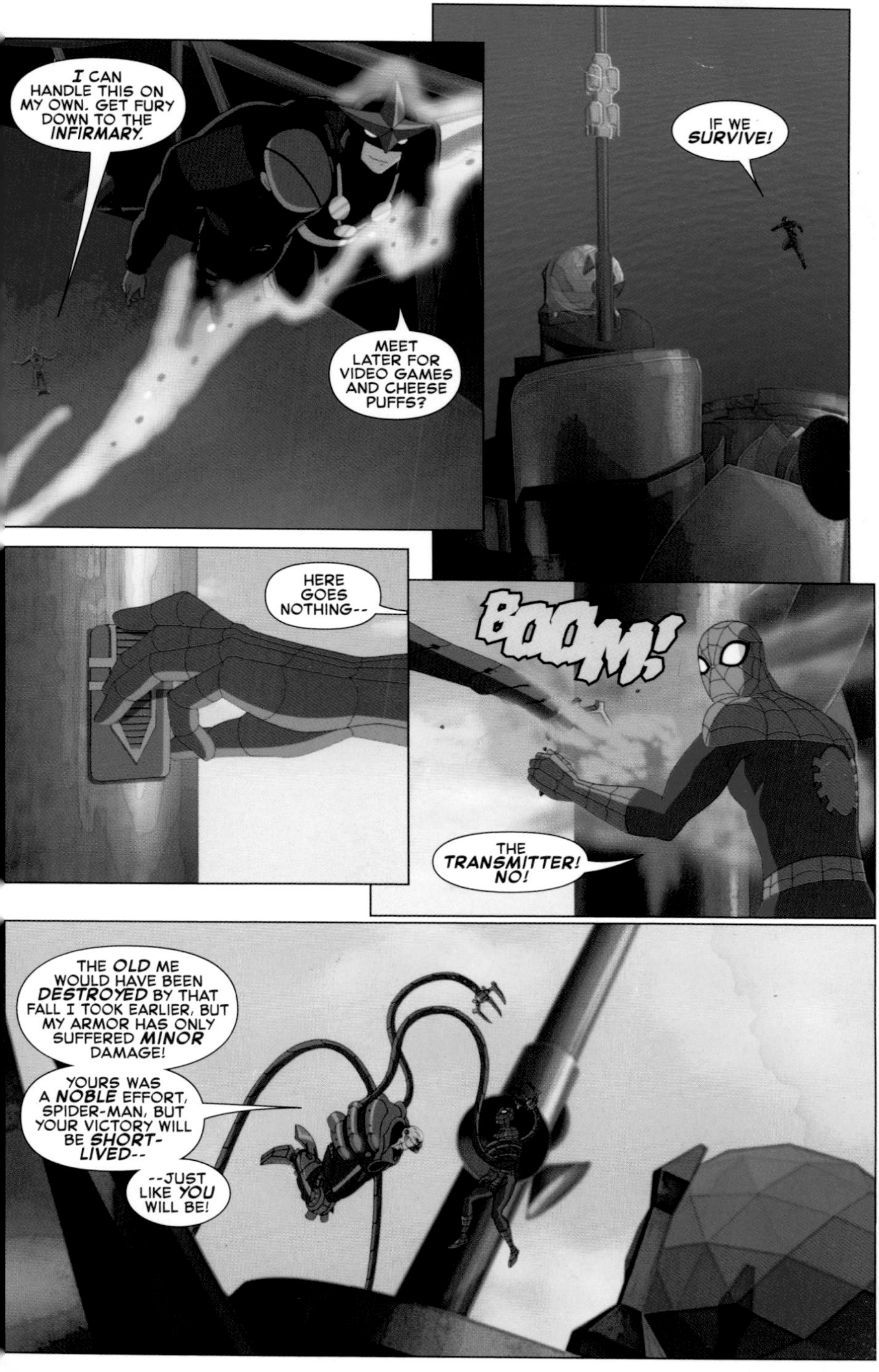
I CAN HANDLE THIS ON MY OWN. GET FURY DOWN TO THE INFIRMARY.
MEET LATER FOR VIDEO GAMES AND CHEESE PUFFS?
IF WE SURVIVE!
HERE GOES NOTHING--
BOOM!
THE TRANSMITTER! NO!
THE OLD ME WOULD HAVE BEEN DESTROYED BY THAT FALL I TOOK EARLIER, BUT MY ARMOR HAS ONLY SUFFERED MINOR DAMAGE!
YOURS WAS A NOBLE EFFORT, SPIDER-MAN, BUT YOUR VICTORY WILL BE SHORT-LIVED--
--JUST LIKE YOU WILL BE!

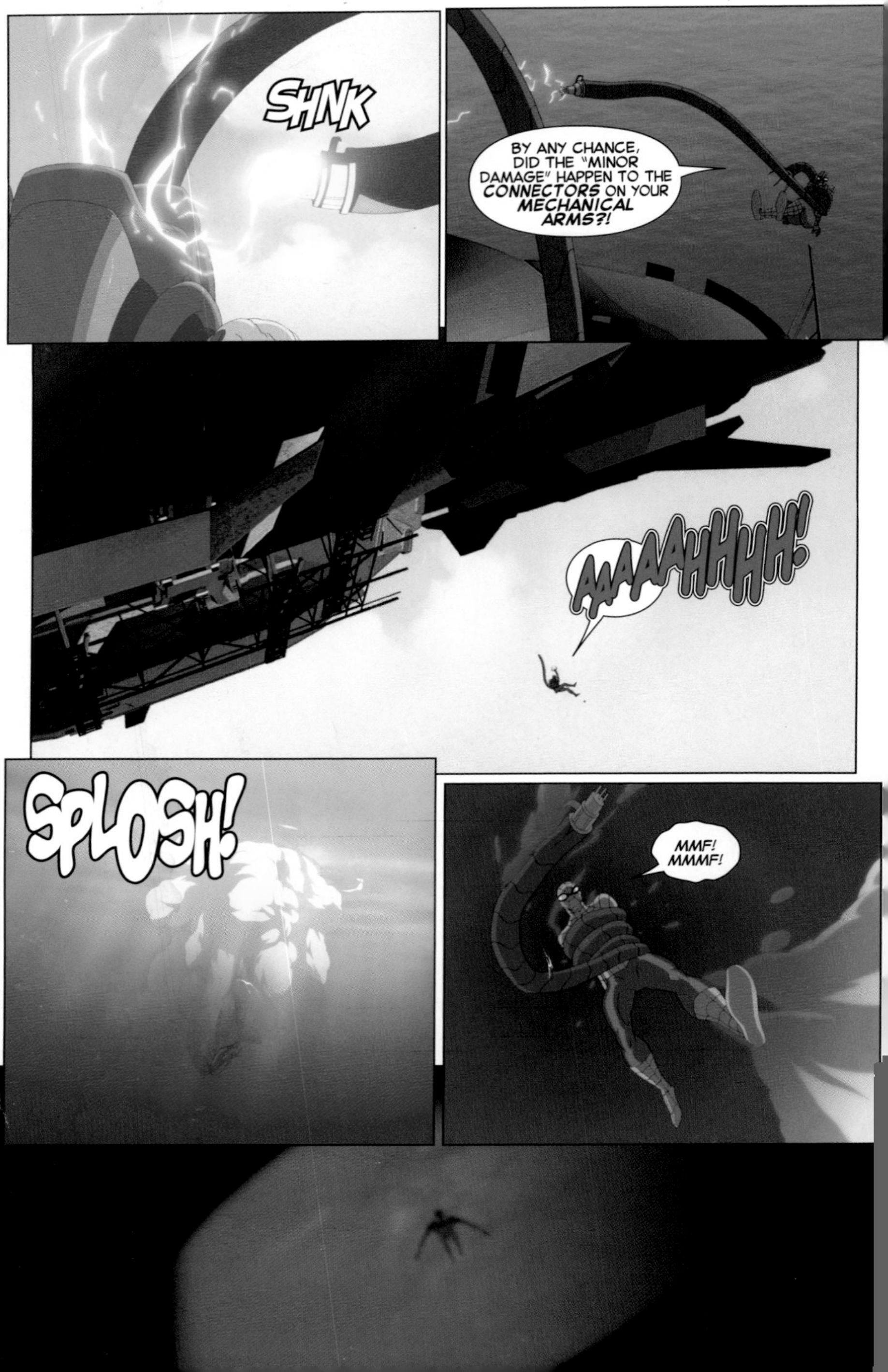
SHNK
BY ANY CHANCE, DID THE "MINOR DAMAGE" HAPPEN TO THE CONNECTORS ON YOUR MECHANICAL ARMS?!
AAAAAHHHHH!
SPLOSH!
MMF! MMMF!

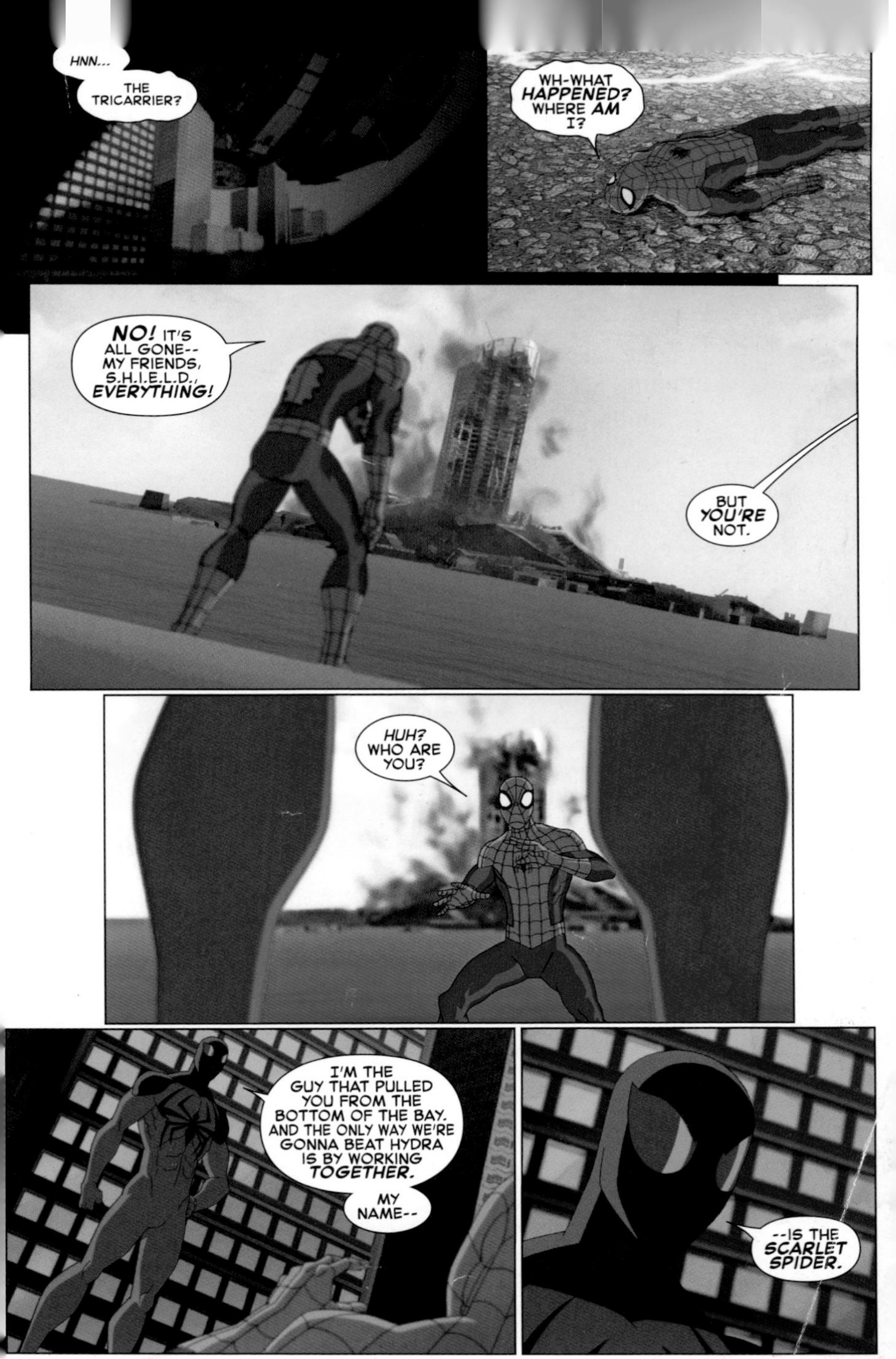
HNN... THE TRICARRIER?
WH-WHAT HAPPENED? WHERE AM I?
NO! IT'S ALL GONE-- MY FRIENDS, S.H.I.E.L.D., EVERYTHING!
BUT YOU'RE NOT.
HUH? WHO ARE YOU?
I'M THE GUY THAT PULLED YOU FROM THE BOTTOM OF THE BAY. AND THE ONLY WAY WE'RE GONNA BEAT HYDRA IS BY WORKING TOGETHER.
MY NAME--
--IS THE SCARLET SPIDER.

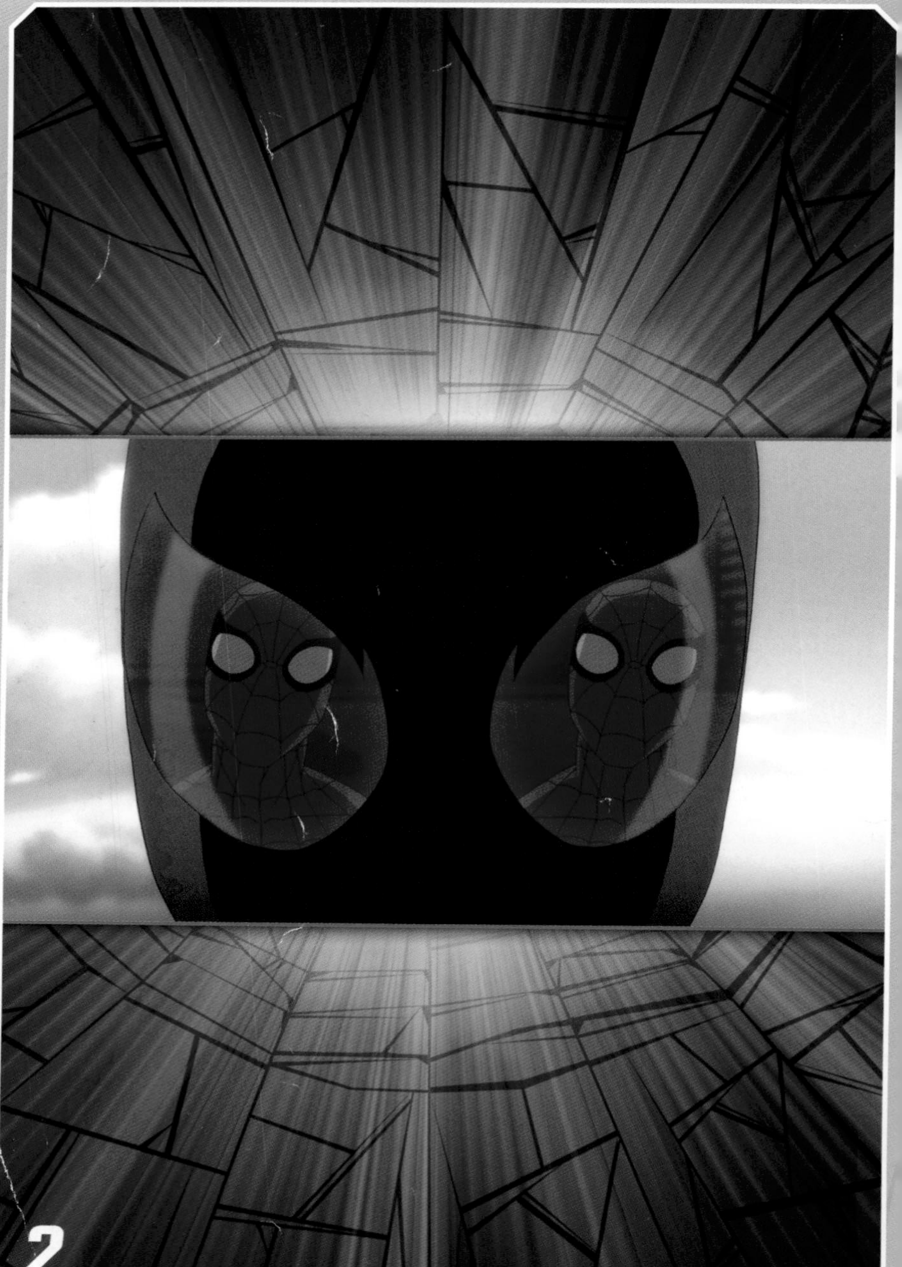

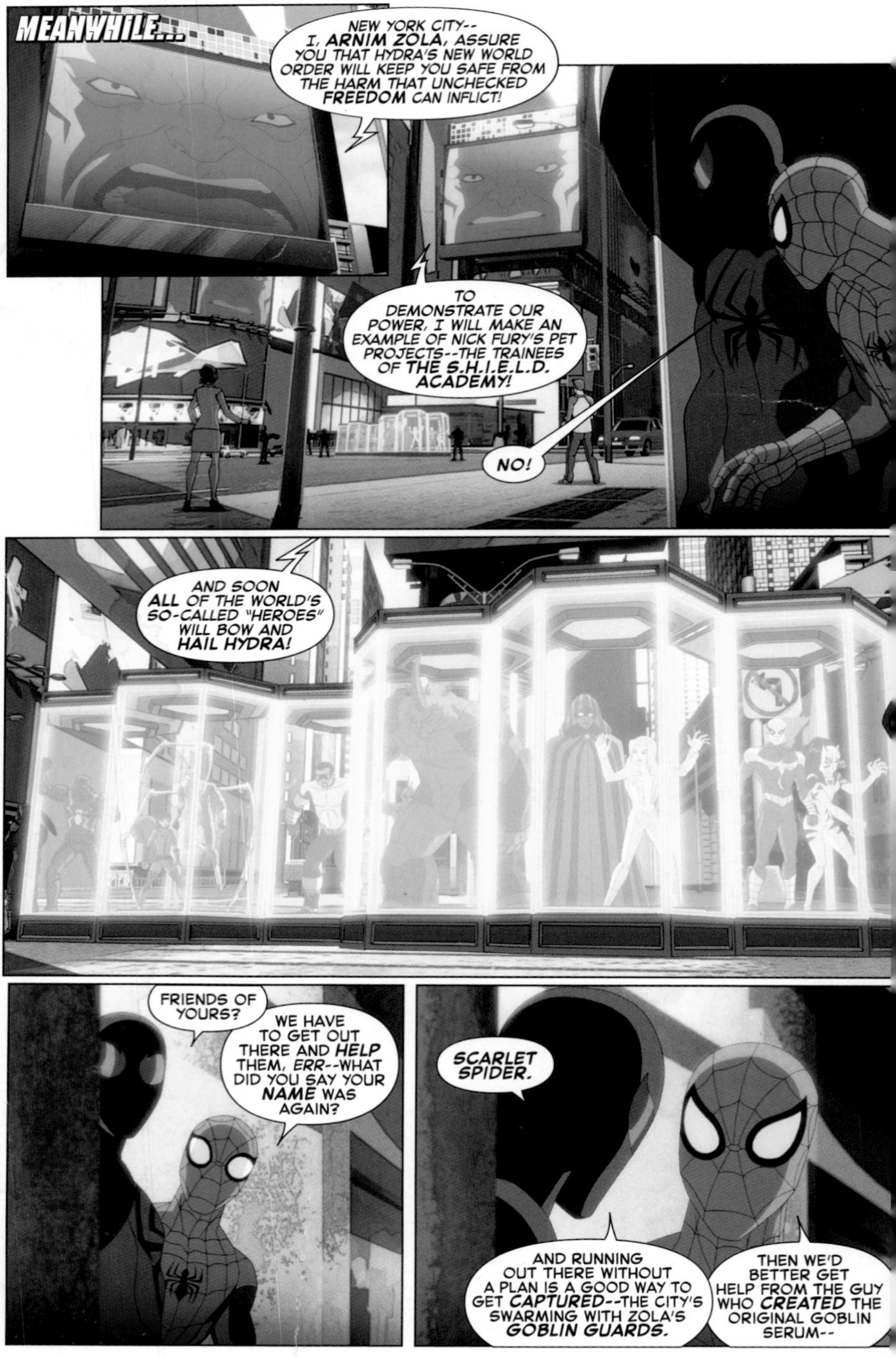
MEANWHILE...
NEW YORK CITY-- I, ARNIM ZOLA, ASSURE YOU THAT HYDRA'S NEW WORLD ORDER WILL KEEP YOU SAFE FROM THE HARM THAT UNCHECKED FREEDOM CAN INFLICT!
TO DEMONSTRATE OUR POWER, I WILL MAKE AN EXAMPLE OF NICK FURY'S PET PROJECTS--THE TRAINEES OF THE S.H.I.E.L.D. ACADEMY!
NO!
AND SOON ALL OF THE WORLD'S SO-CALLED "HEROES" WILL BOW AND HAIL HYDRA!
FRIENDS OF YOURS?
WE HAVE TO GET OUT THERE AND HELP THEM, ERR--WHAT DID YOU SAY YOUR NAME WAS AGAIN?
SCARLET SPIDER.
AND RUNNING OUT THERE WITHOUT A PLAN IS A GOOD WAY TO GET CAPTURED--THE CITY'S SWARMING WITH ZOLA'S GOBLIN GUARDS.
THEN WE'D BETTER GET HELP FROM THE GUY WHO CREATED THE ORIGINAL GOBLIN SERUM--

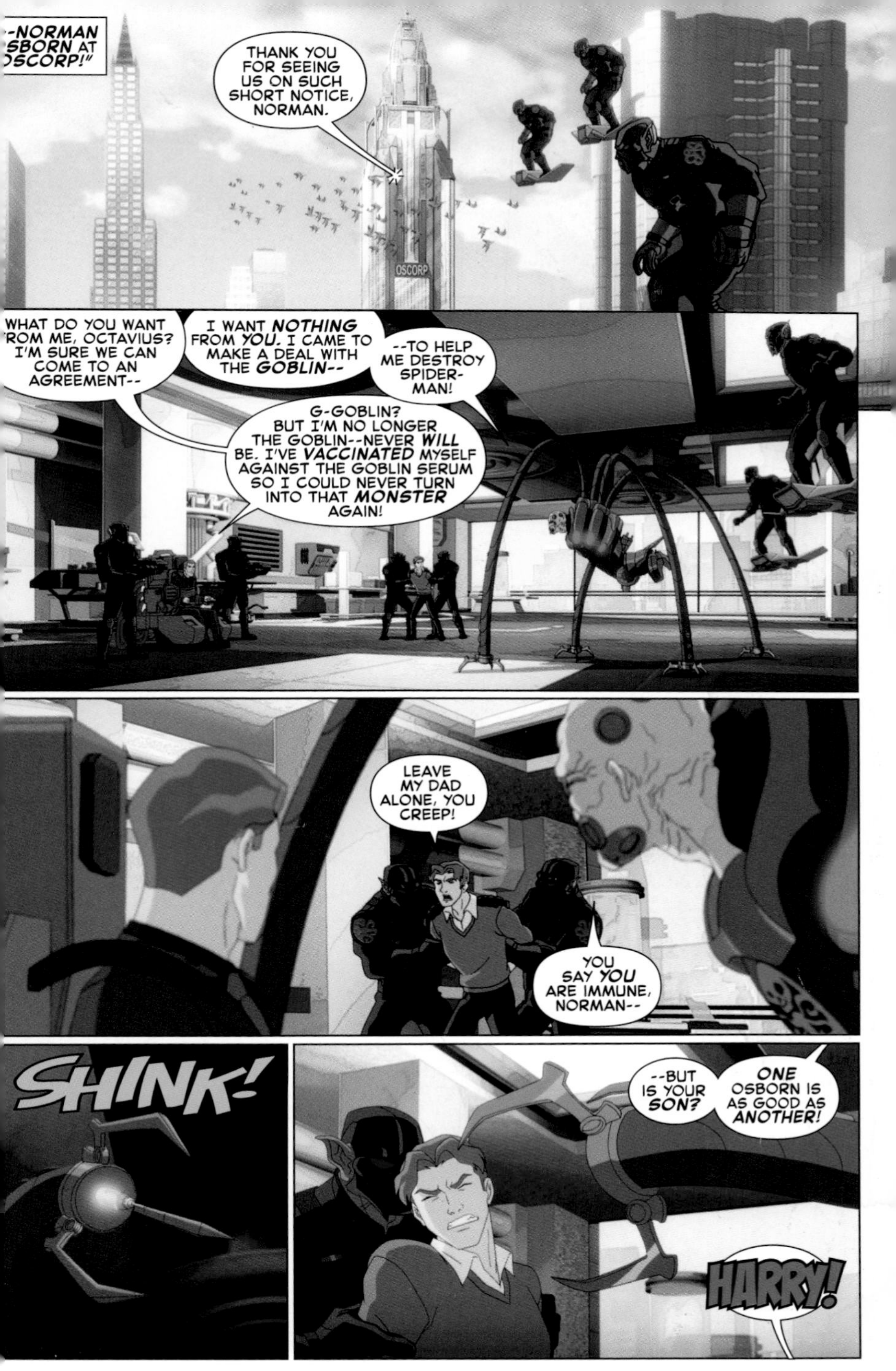
-NORMAN OSBORN AT OSCORP!"
THANK YOU FOR SEEING US ON SUCH SHORT NOTICE, NORMAN.
OSCORP
WHAT DO YOU WANT FROM ME, OCTAVIUS? I'M SURE WE CAN COME TO AN AGREEMENT--
I WANT NOTHING FROM YOU. I CAME TO MAKE A DEAL WITH THE GOBLIN--
--TO HELP ME DESTROY SPIDER-MAN!
G-GOBLIN? BUT I'M NO LONGER THE GOBLIN--NEVER WILL BE. I'VE VACCINATED MYSELF AGAINST THE GOBLIN SERUM SO I COULD NEVER TURN INTO THAT MONSTER AGAIN!
LEAVE MY DAD ALONE, YOU CREEP!
YOU SAY YOU ARE IMMUNE, NORMAN--
SHINK!
--BUT IS YOUR SON?
ONE OSBORN IS AS GOOD AS ANOTHER!
HARRY!

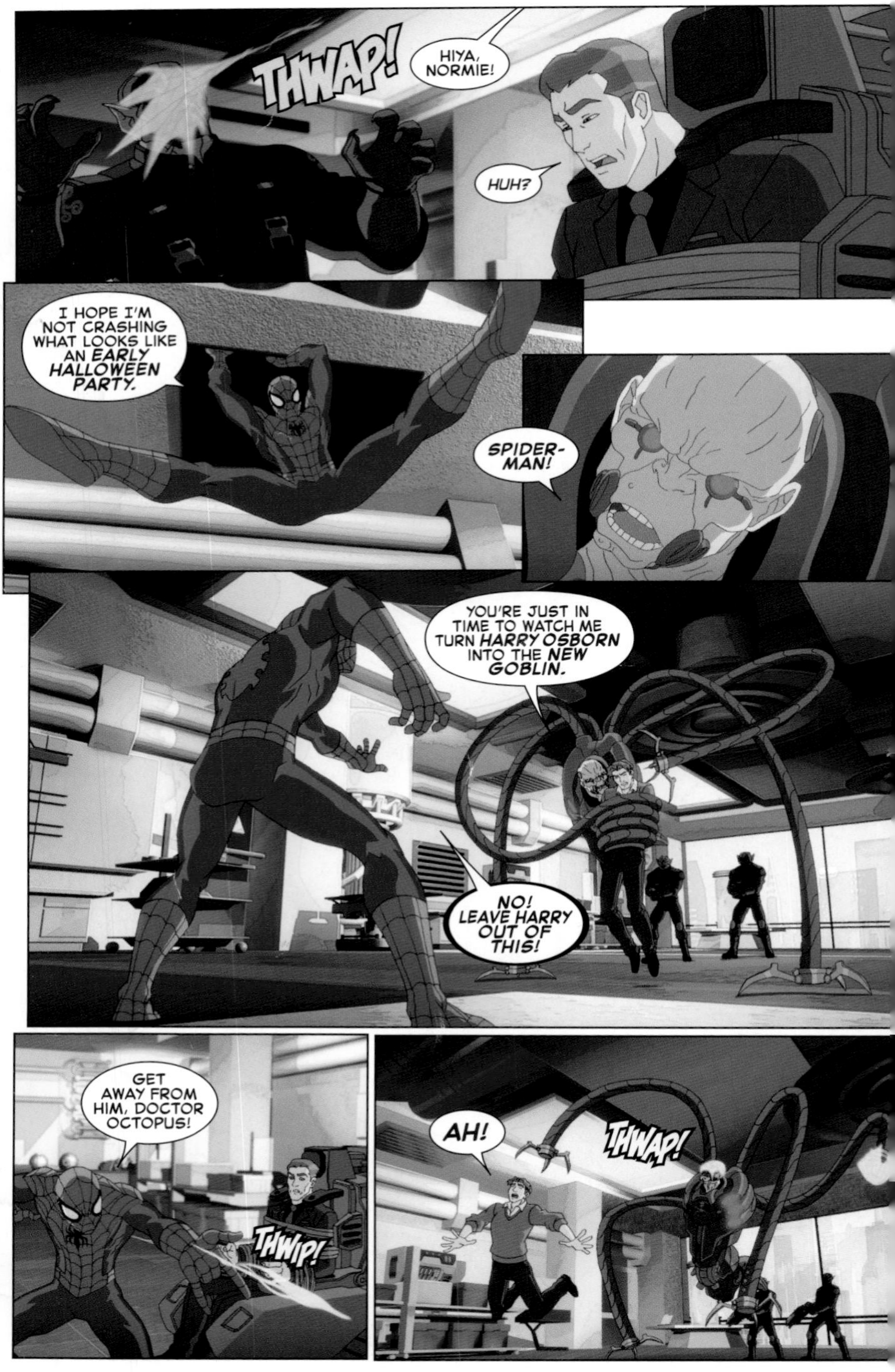
THWAP!
HIYA, NORMIE!
HUH?
I HOPE I'M NOT CRASHING WHAT LOOKS LIKE AN EARLY HALLOWEEN PARTY.
SPIDER-MAN!
YOU'RE JUST IN TIME TO WATCH ME TURN HARRY OSBORN INTO THE NEW GOBLIN.
NO! LEAVE HARRY OUT OF THIS!
GET AWAY FROM HIM, DOCTOR OCTOPUS!
THWIP!
AH!
THWAP!

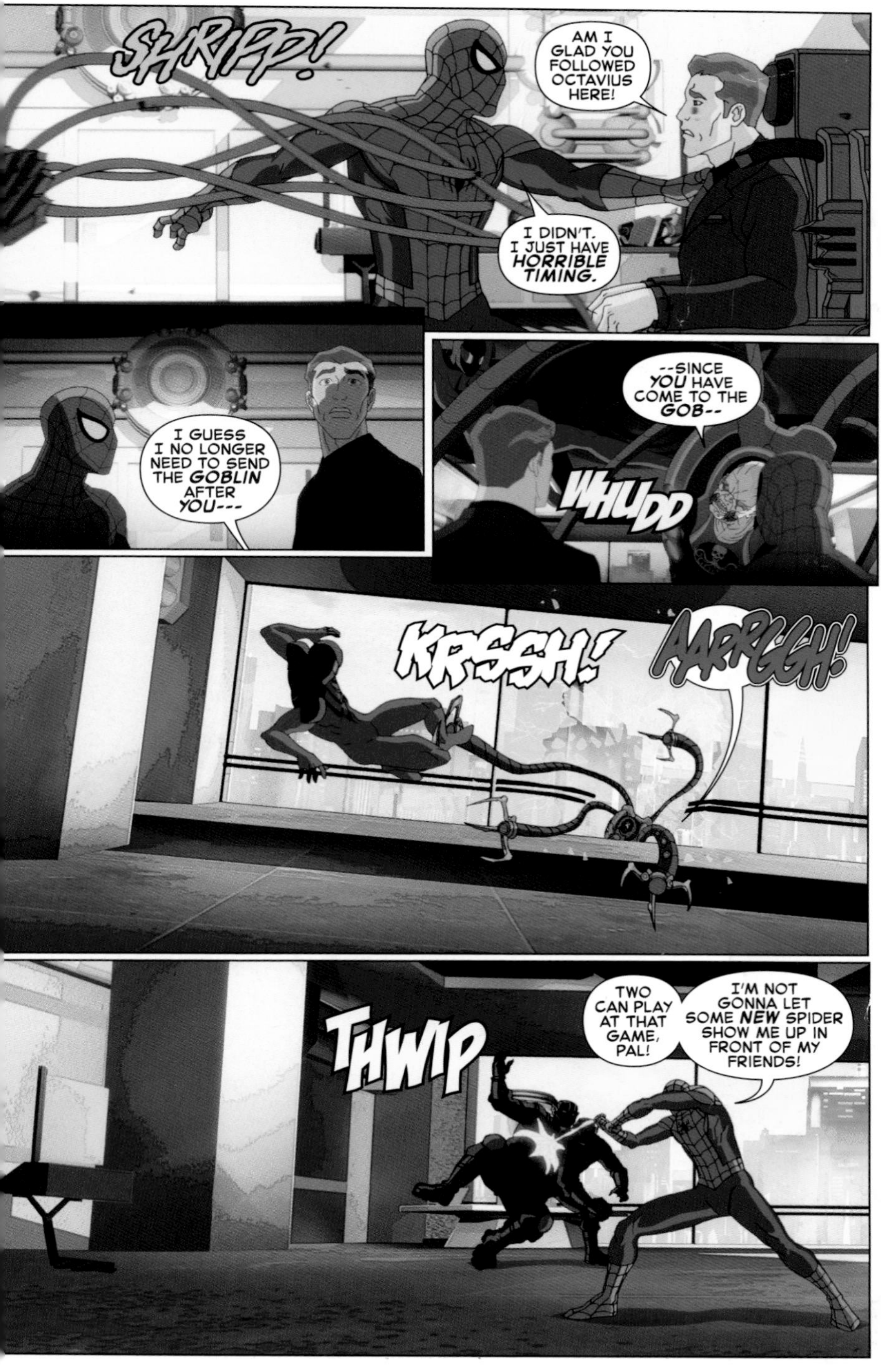
SHRIPP!
AM I GLAD YOU FOLLOWED OCTAVIUS HERE!
I DIDN'T. I JUST HAVE HORRIBLE TIMING.
I GUESS I NO LONGER NEED TO SEND THE GOBLIN AFTER YOU---
--SINCE YOU HAVE COME TO THE GOB--
WHUDD
KRSSH!
AARRGGH!
THWIP
TWO CAN PLAY AT THAT GAME, PAL!
I'M NOT GONNA LET SOME NEW SPIDER SHOW ME UP IN FRONT OF MY FRIENDS!

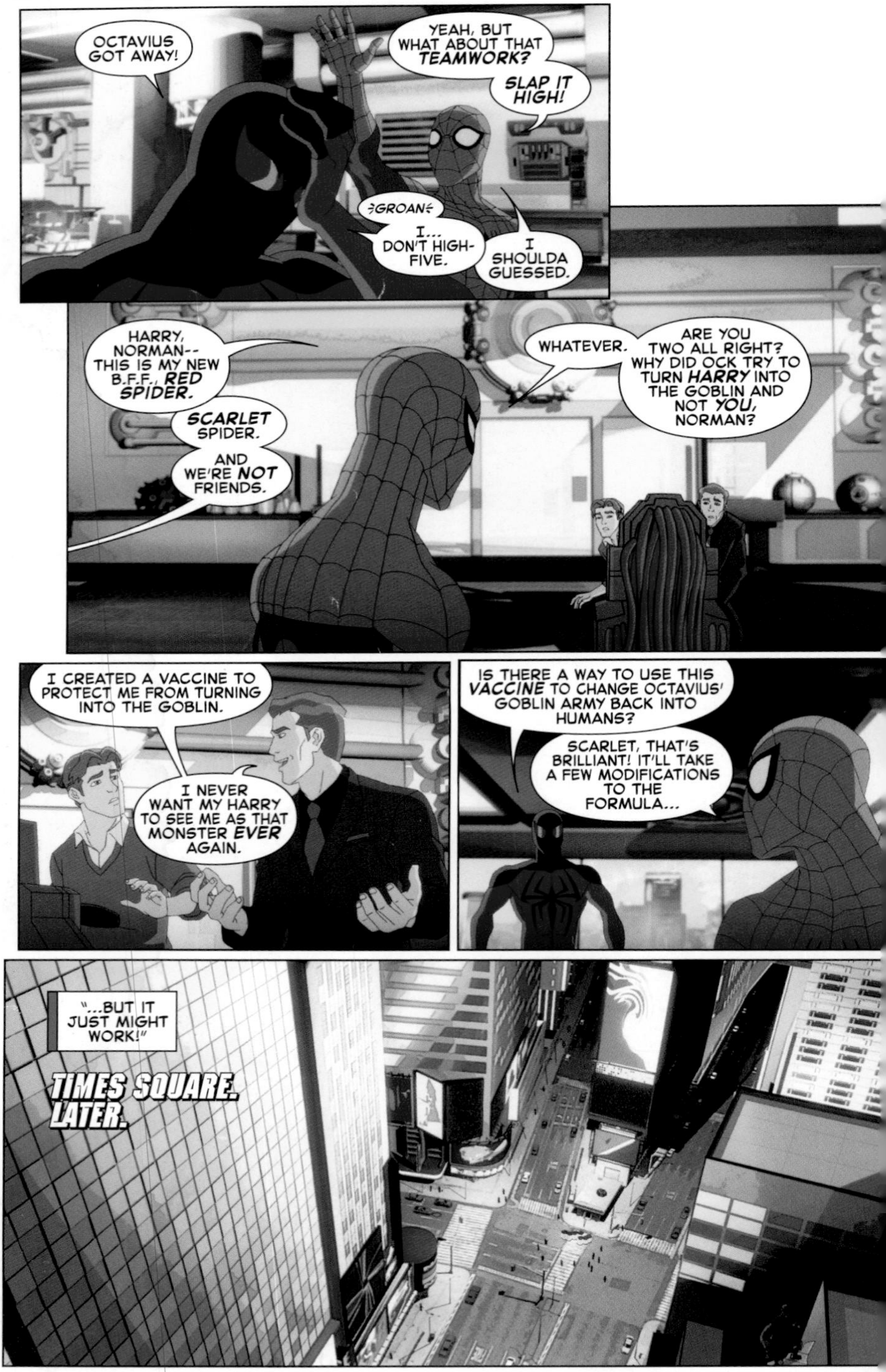
OCTAVIUS GOT AWAY!
YEAH, BUT WHAT ABOUT THAT TEAMWORK?
SLAP IT HIGH!
≯GROAN≮
I... DON'T HIGH-FIVE.
I SHOULDA GUESSED.
HARRY, NORMAN-- THIS IS MY NEW B.F.F., RED SPIDER.
SCARLET SPIDER.
AND WE'RE NOT FRIENDS.
WHATEVER.
ARE YOU TWO ALL RIGHT? WHY DID OCK TRY TO TURN HARRY INTO THE GOBLIN AND NOT YOU, NORMAN?
I CREATED A VACCINE TO PROTECT ME FROM TURNING INTO THE GOBLIN.
I NEVER WANT MY HARRY TO SEE ME AS THAT MONSTER EVER AGAIN.
IS THERE A WAY TO USE THIS VACCINE TO CHANGE OCTAVIUS' GOBLIN ARMY BACK INTO HUMANS?
SCARLET, THAT'S BRILLIANT! IT'LL TAKE A FEW MODIFICATIONS TO THE FORMULA...
"...BUT IT JUST MIGHT WORK!"
TIMES SQUARE. LATER.

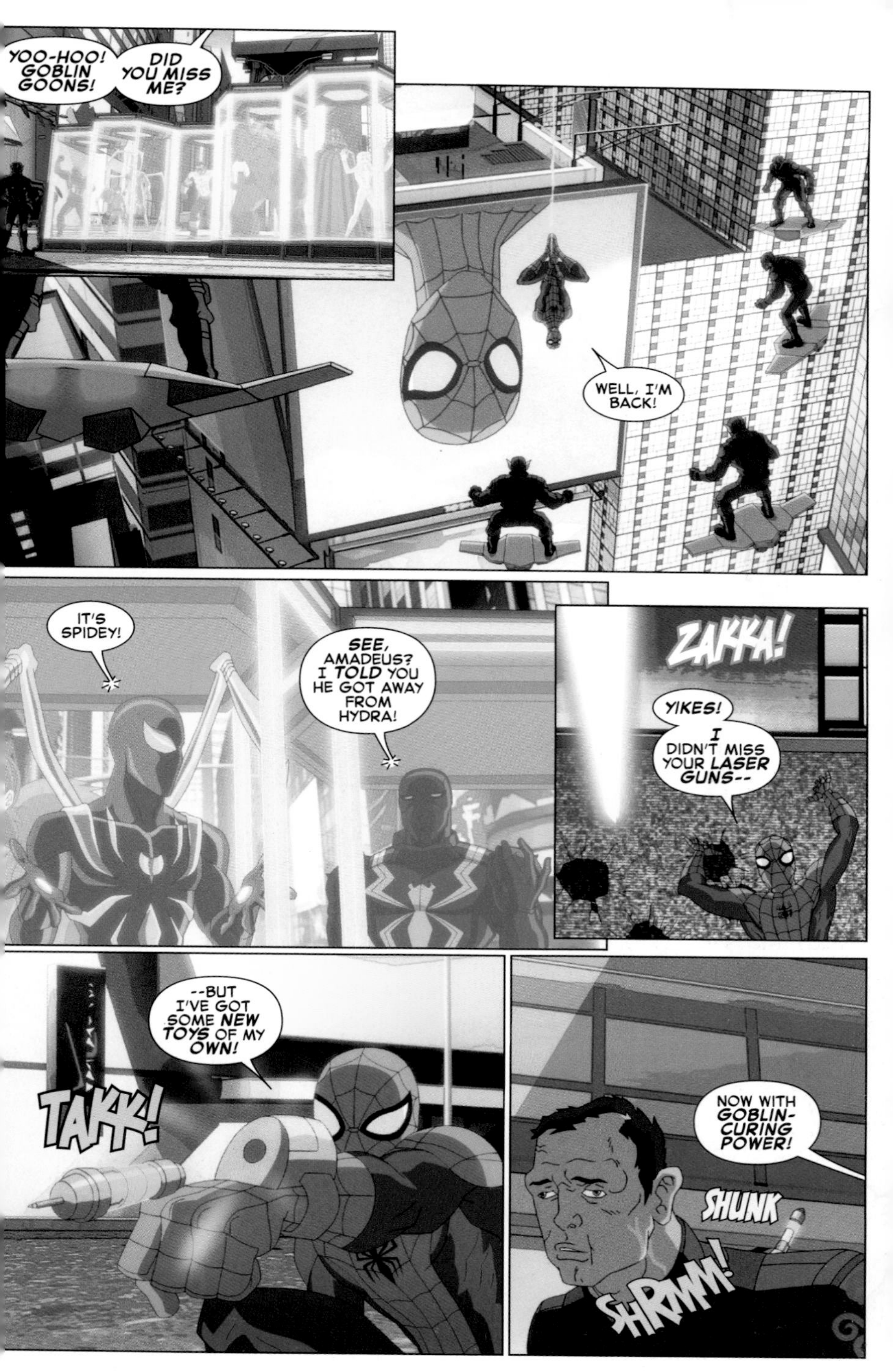
YOO-HOO! GOBLIN GOONS!
DID YOU MISS ME?
WELL, I'M BACK!
IT'S SPIDEY!
SEE, AMADEUS? I TOLD YOU HE GOT AWAY FROM HYDRA!
ZAKKA!
YIKES!
I DIDN'T MISS YOUR LASER GUNS--
--BUT I'VE GOT SOME NEW TOYS OF MY OWN!
TAKK!
NOW WITH GOBLIN-CURING POWER!
SHUNK
SHRMM!

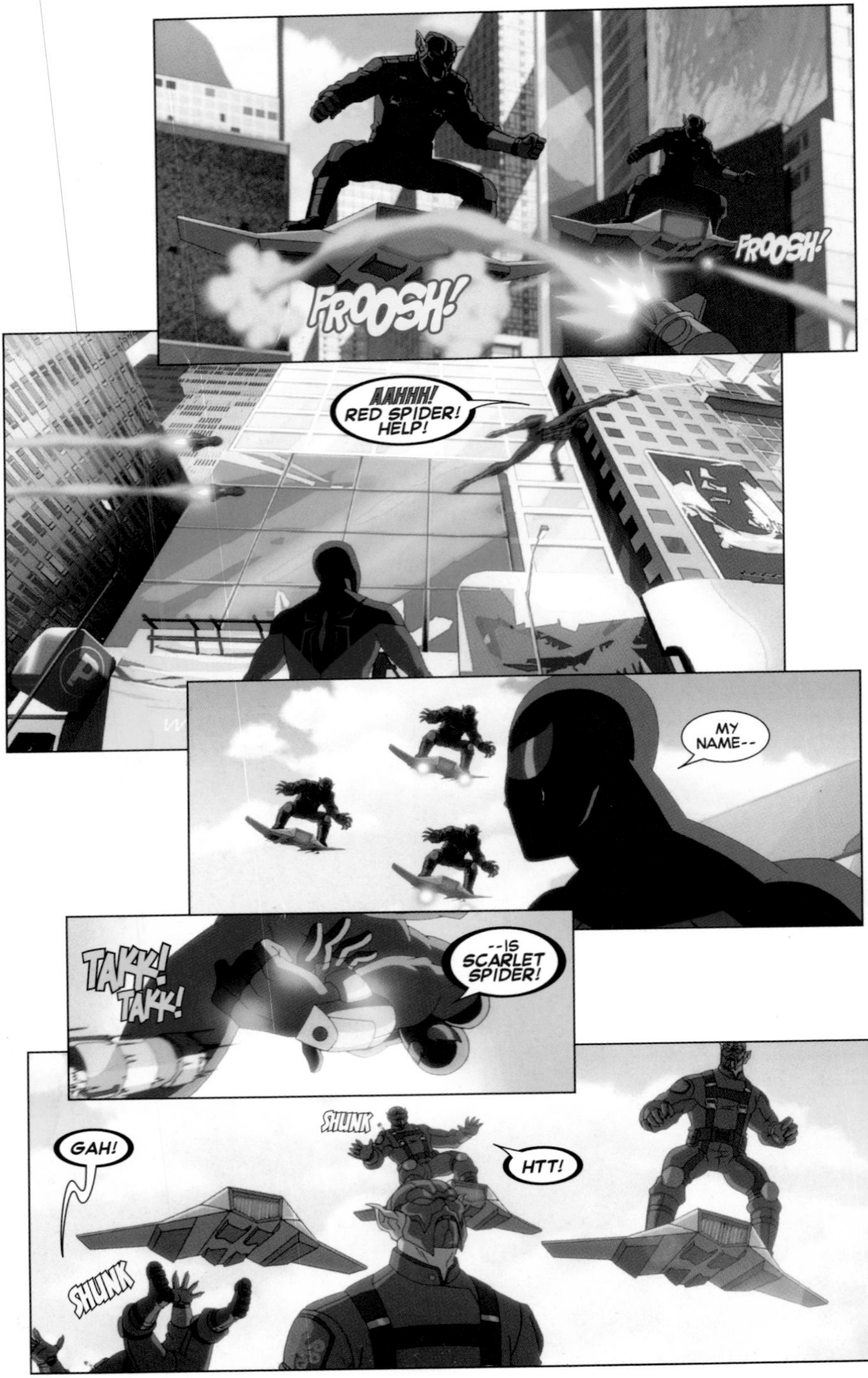
FROOSH!
FROOSH!
AAHHH! RED SPIDER! HELP!
MY NAME--
TAKK! TAKK!
--IS SCARLET SPIDER!
SHUNK
GAH!
HTT!
SHUNK

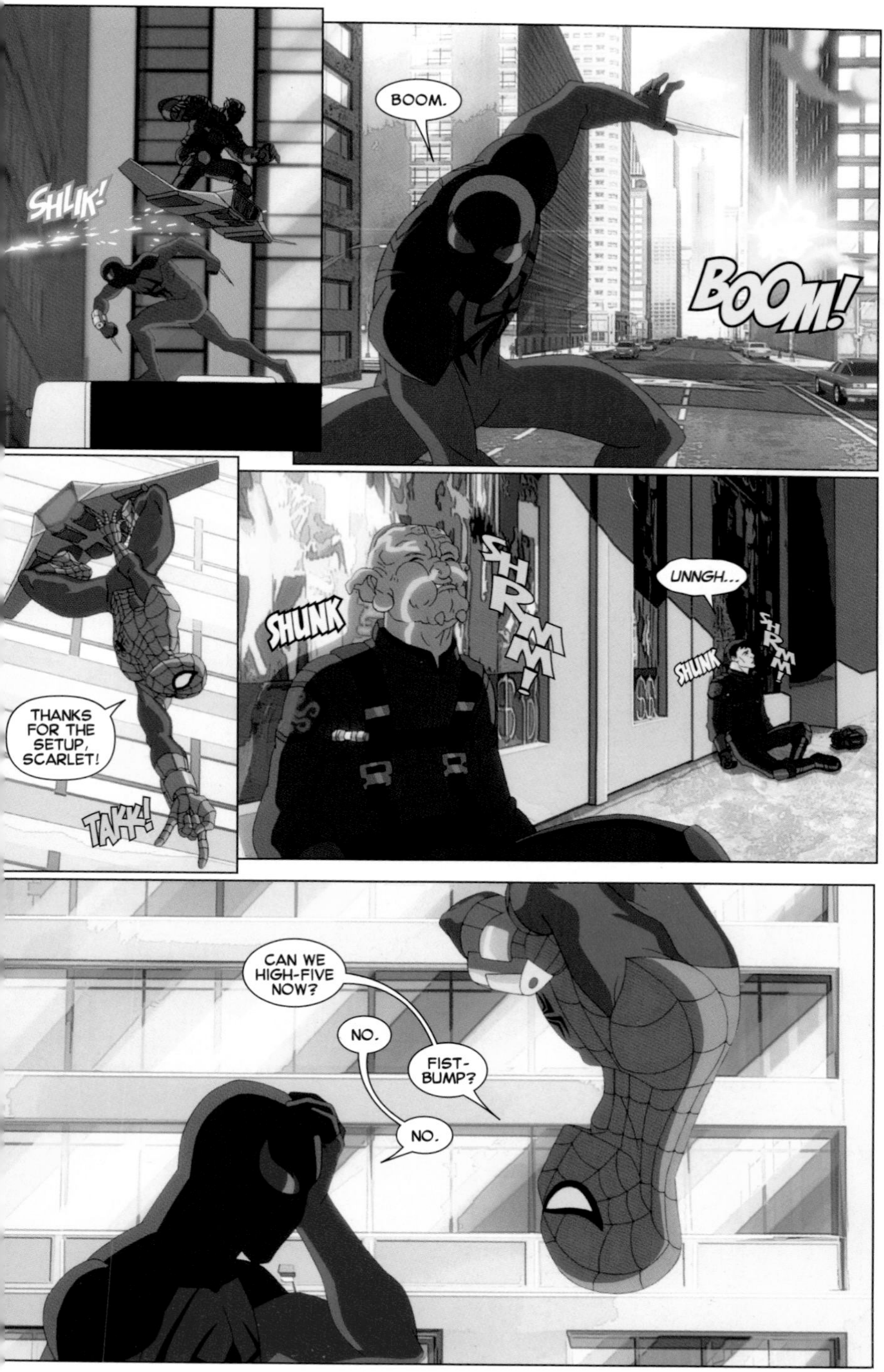

SHLIK!
BOOM.
BOOM!
THANKS FOR THE SETUP, SCARLET!
TAKK!
SHUNK
SHRMM!
UNNGH...
SHUNK
SHRMM!
CAN WE HIGH-FIVE NOW?
NO.
FIST-BUMP?
NO.

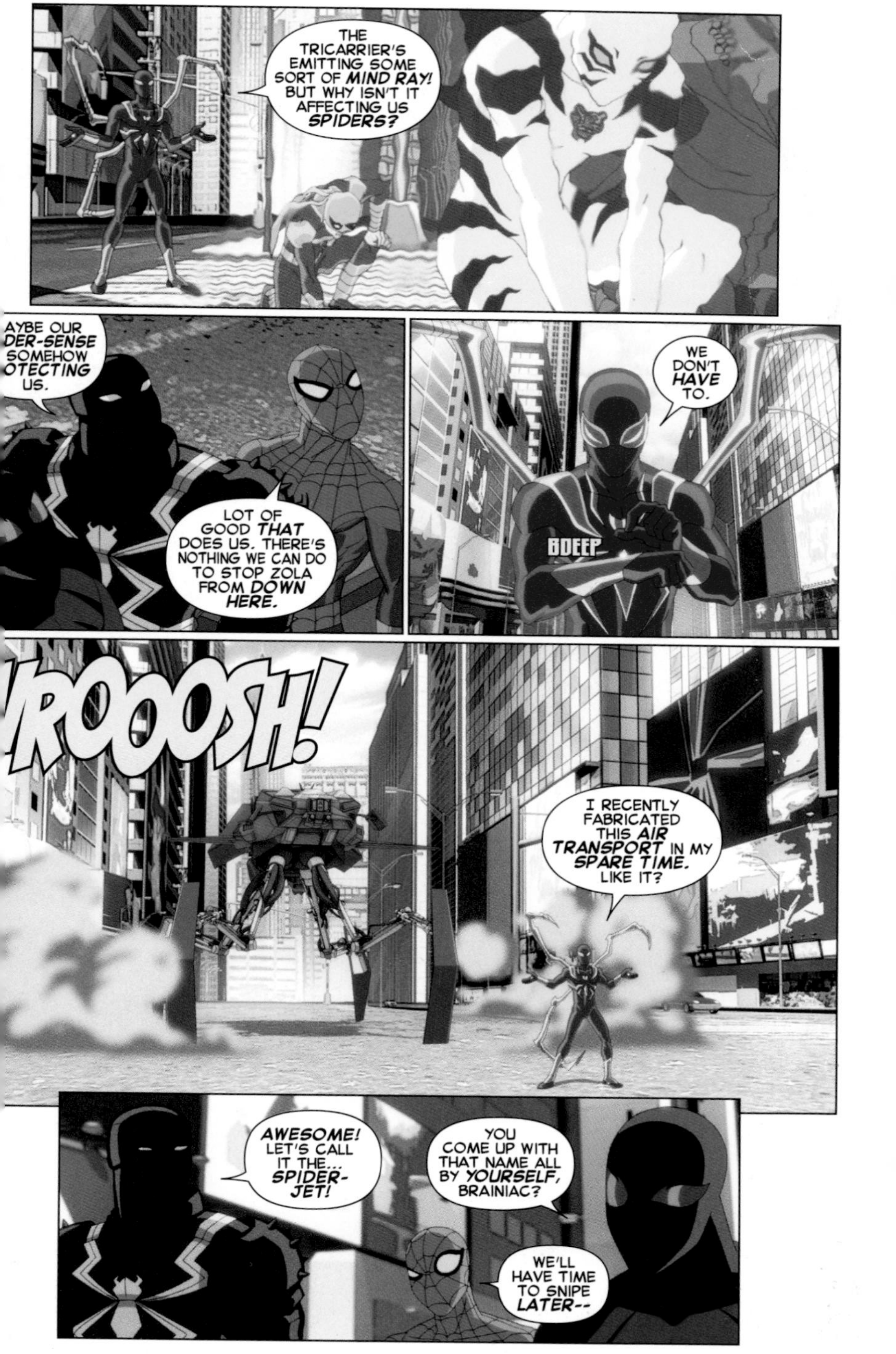

THE TRICARRIER'S EMITTING SOME SORT OF MIND RAY! BUT WHY ISN'T IT AFFECTING US SPIDERS?
AYBE OUR DER-SENSE SOMEHOW OTECTING US.
LOT OF GOOD THAT DOES US. THERE'S NOTHING WE CAN DO TO STOP ZOLA FROM DOWN HERE.
WE DON'T HAVE TO.
BDEEP
ROOOSH!
I RECENTLY FABRICATED THIS AIR TRANSPORT IN MY SPARE TIME. LIKE IT?
AWESOME! LET'S CALL IT THE... SPIDER-JET!
YOU COME UP WITH THAT NAME ALL BY YOURSELF, BRAINIAC?
WE'LL HAVE TIME TO SNIPE LATER--

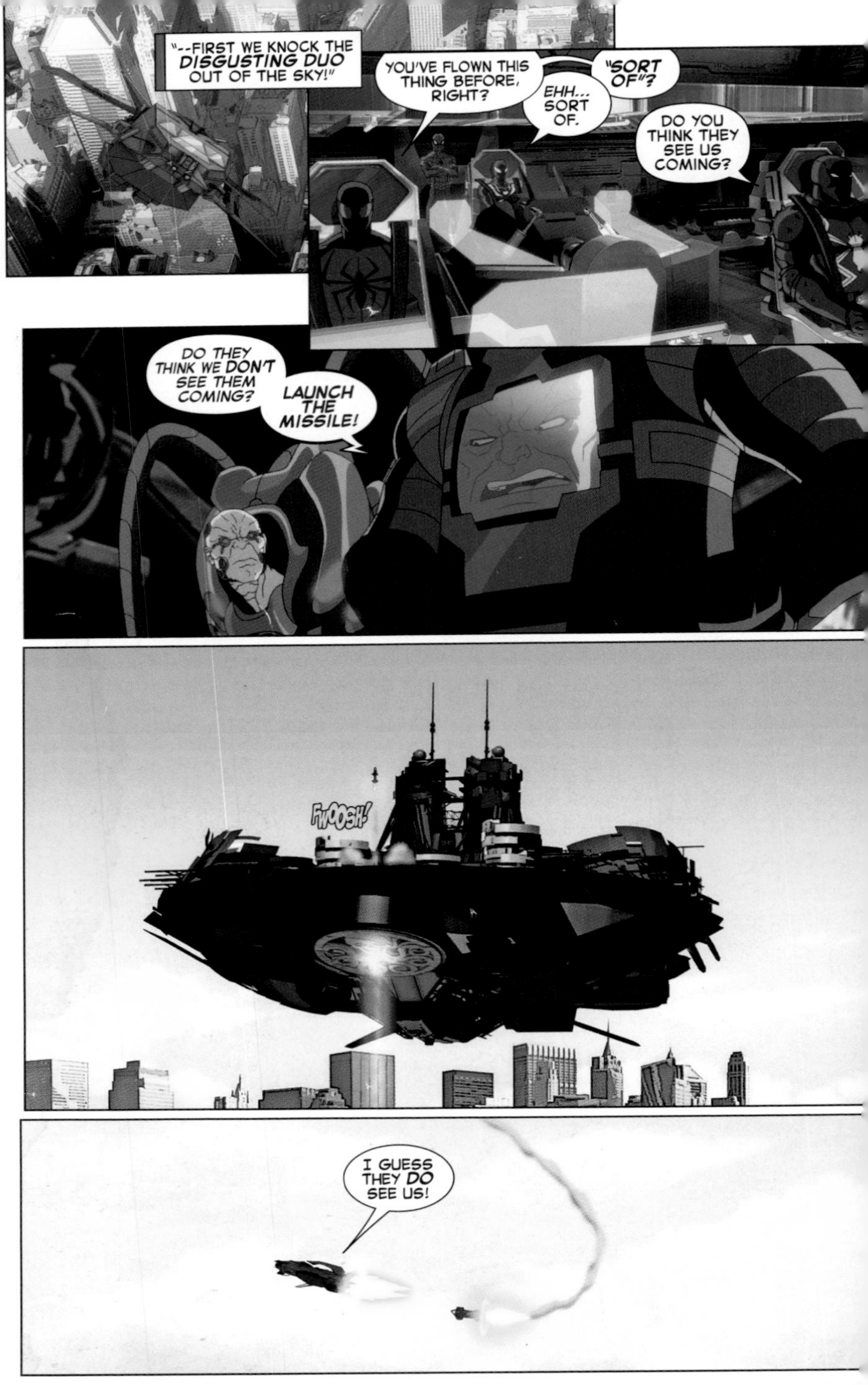

"--FIRST WE KNOCK THE DISGUSTING DUO OUT OF THE SKY!"
YOU'VE FLOWN THIS THING BEFORE, RIGHT?
EHH... SORT OF.
"SORT OF"?
DO YOU THINK THEY SEE US COMING?
DO THEY THINK WE DON'T SEE THEM COMING?
LAUNCH THE MISSILE!
FWOOSH!
I GUESS THEY DO SEE US!

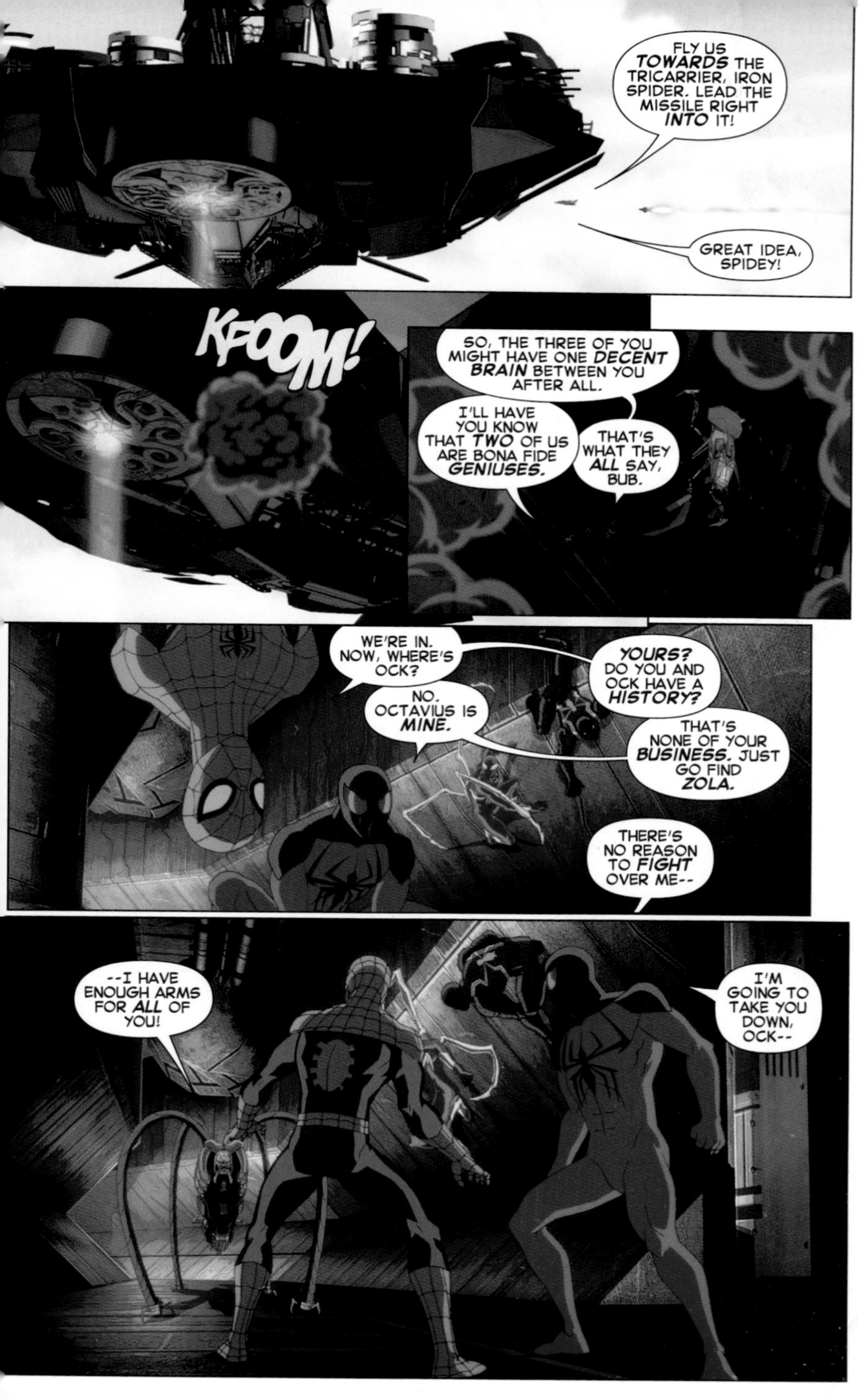
FLY US TOWARDS THE TRICARRIER, IRON SPIDER. LEAD THE MISSILE RIGHT INTO IT!
GREAT IDEA, SPIDEY!
KFOOM!
SO, THE THREE OF YOU MIGHT HAVE ONE DECENT BRAIN BETWEEN YOU AFTER ALL.
I'LL HAVE YOU KNOW THAT TWO OF US ARE BONA FIDE GENIUSES.
THAT'S WHAT THEY ALL SAY, BUB.
WE'RE IN. NOW, WHERE'S OCK?
NO. OCTAVIUS IS MINE.
YOURS? DO YOU AND OCK HAVE A HISTORY?
THAT'S NONE OF YOUR BUSINESS. JUST GO FIND ZOLA.
THERE'S NO REASON TO FIGHT OVER ME--
--I HAVE ENOUGH ARMS FOR ALL OF YOU!
I'M GOING TO TAKE YOU DOWN, OCK--

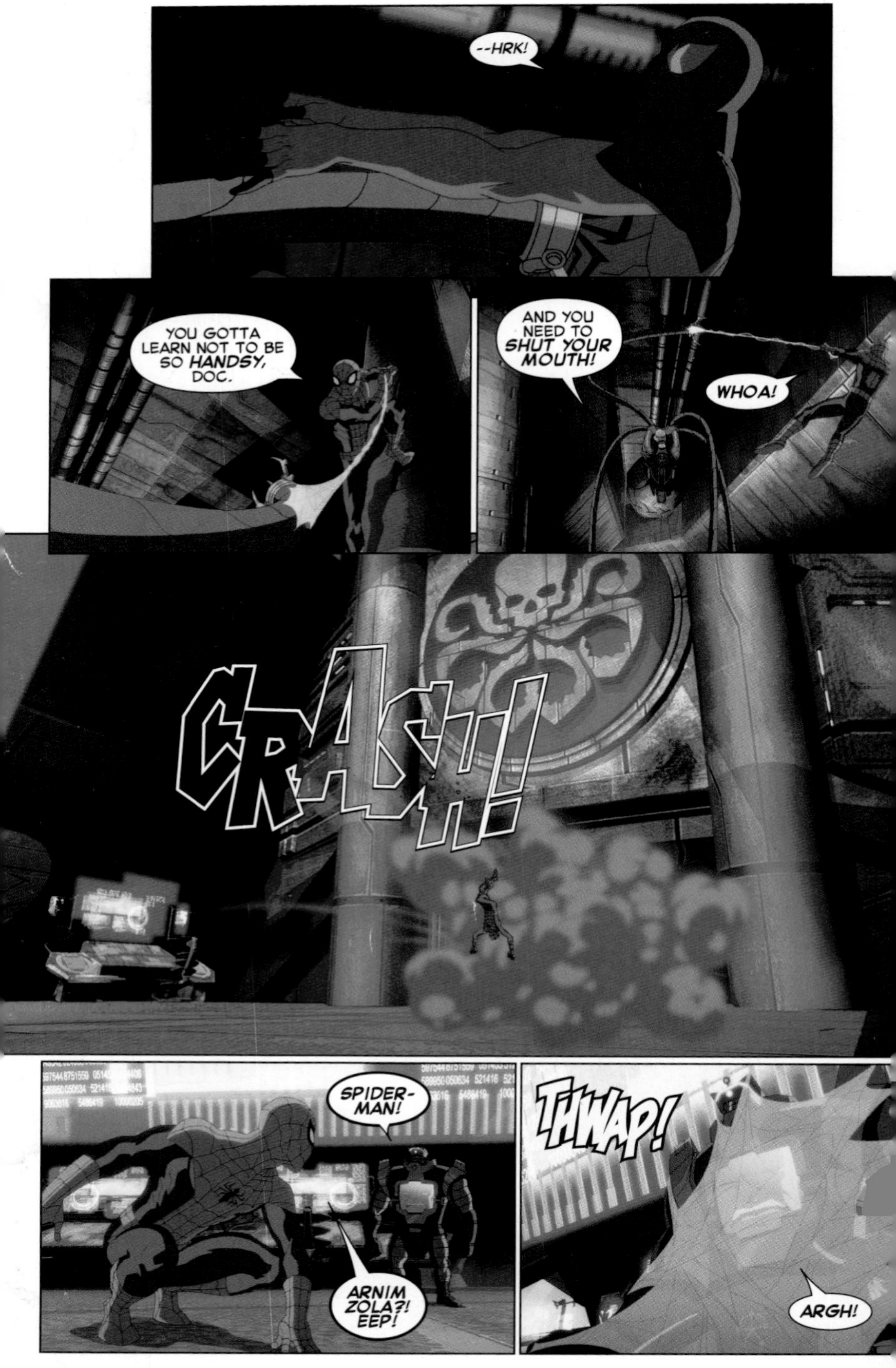
--HRK!
YOU GOTTA LEARN NOT TO BE SO HANDSY, DOC.
AND YOU NEED TO SHUT YOUR MOUTH!
WHOA!
CRASH!
SPIDER-MAN!
ARNIM ZOLA?! EEP!
THWAP!
ARGH!

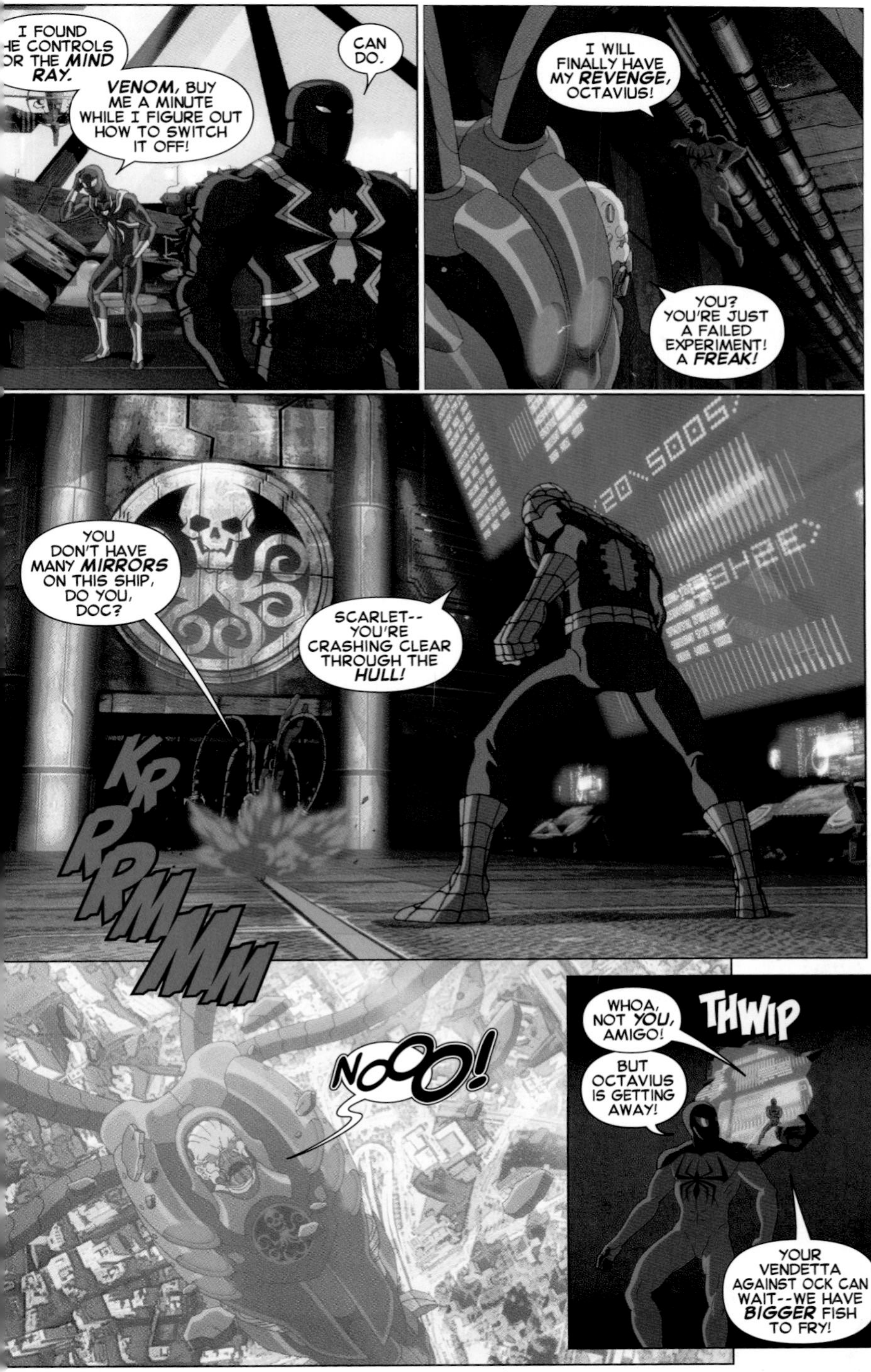
I FOUND HE CONTROLS OR THE MIND RAY.
VENOM, BUY ME A MINUTE WHILE I FIGURE OUT HOW TO SWITCH IT OFF!
CAN DO.
I WILL FINALLY HAVE MY REVENGE, OCTAVIUS!
YOU? YOU'RE JUST A FAILED EXPERIMENT! A FREAK!
YOU DON'T HAVE MANY MIRRORS ON THIS SHIP, DO YOU, DOC?
SCARLET-- YOU'RE CRASHING CLEAR THROUGH THE HULL!
KRRRMMMM
NOOOO!
WHOA, NOT YOU, AMIGO!
THWIP
BUT OCTAVIUS IS GETTING AWAY!
YOUR VENDETTA AGAINST OCK CAN WAIT--WE HAVE BIGGER FISH TO FRY!

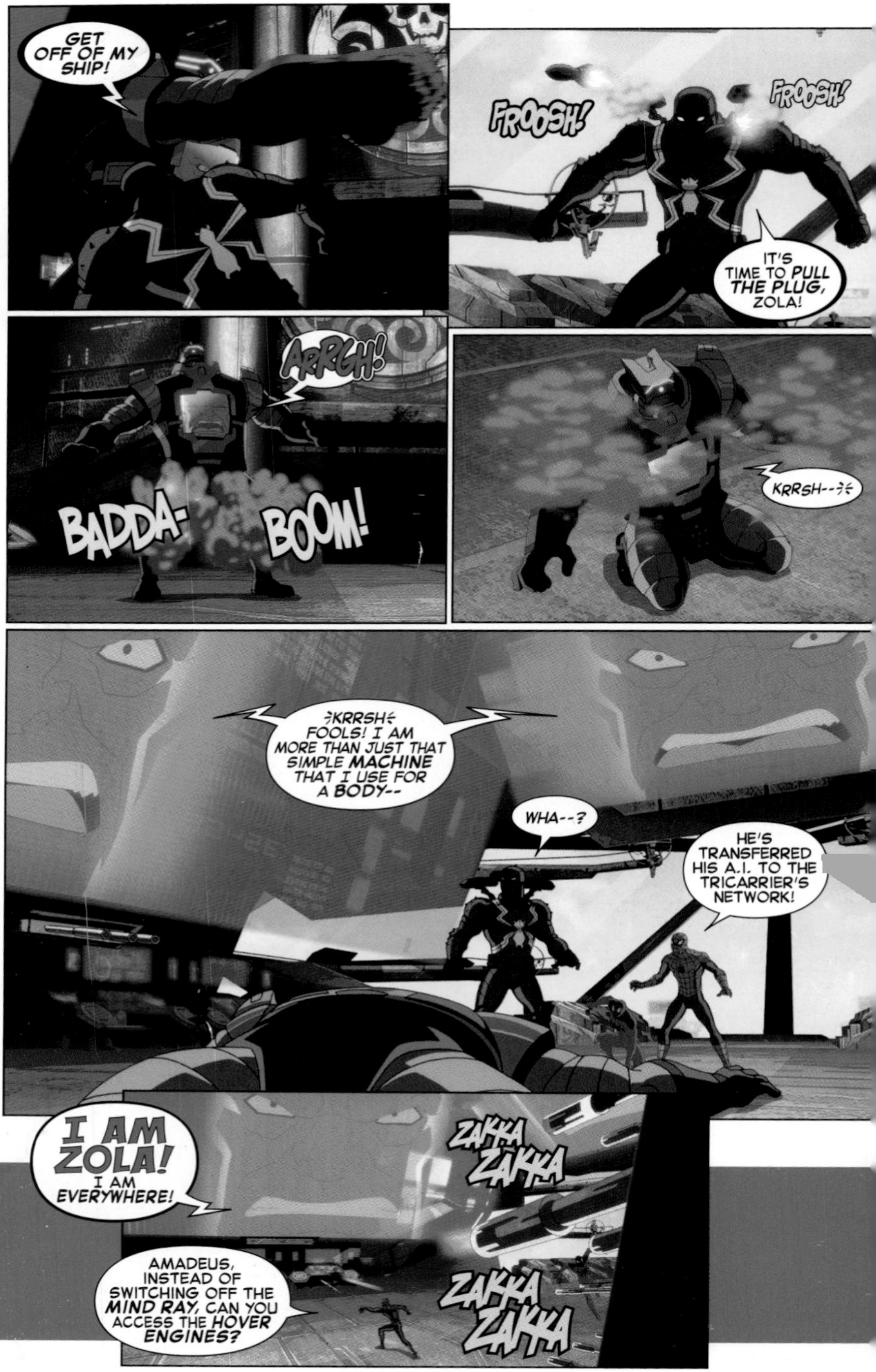

GET OFF OF MY SHIP!
FROOSH!
FROOSH!
IT'S TIME TO PULL THE PLUG, ZOLA!
ARRGH!
BADDA-
BOOM!
KRRSH--
KRRSH FOOLS! I AM MORE THAN JUST THAT SIMPLE MACHINE THAT I USE FOR A BODY--
WHA--?
HE'S TRANSFERRED HIS A.I. TO THE TRICARRIER'S NETWORK!
I AM ZOLA! I AM EVERYWHERE!
ZAKKA ZAKKA
AMADEUS, INSTEAD OF SWITCHING OFF THE MIND RAY, CAN YOU ACCESS THE HOVER ENGINES?
ZAKKA ZAKKA

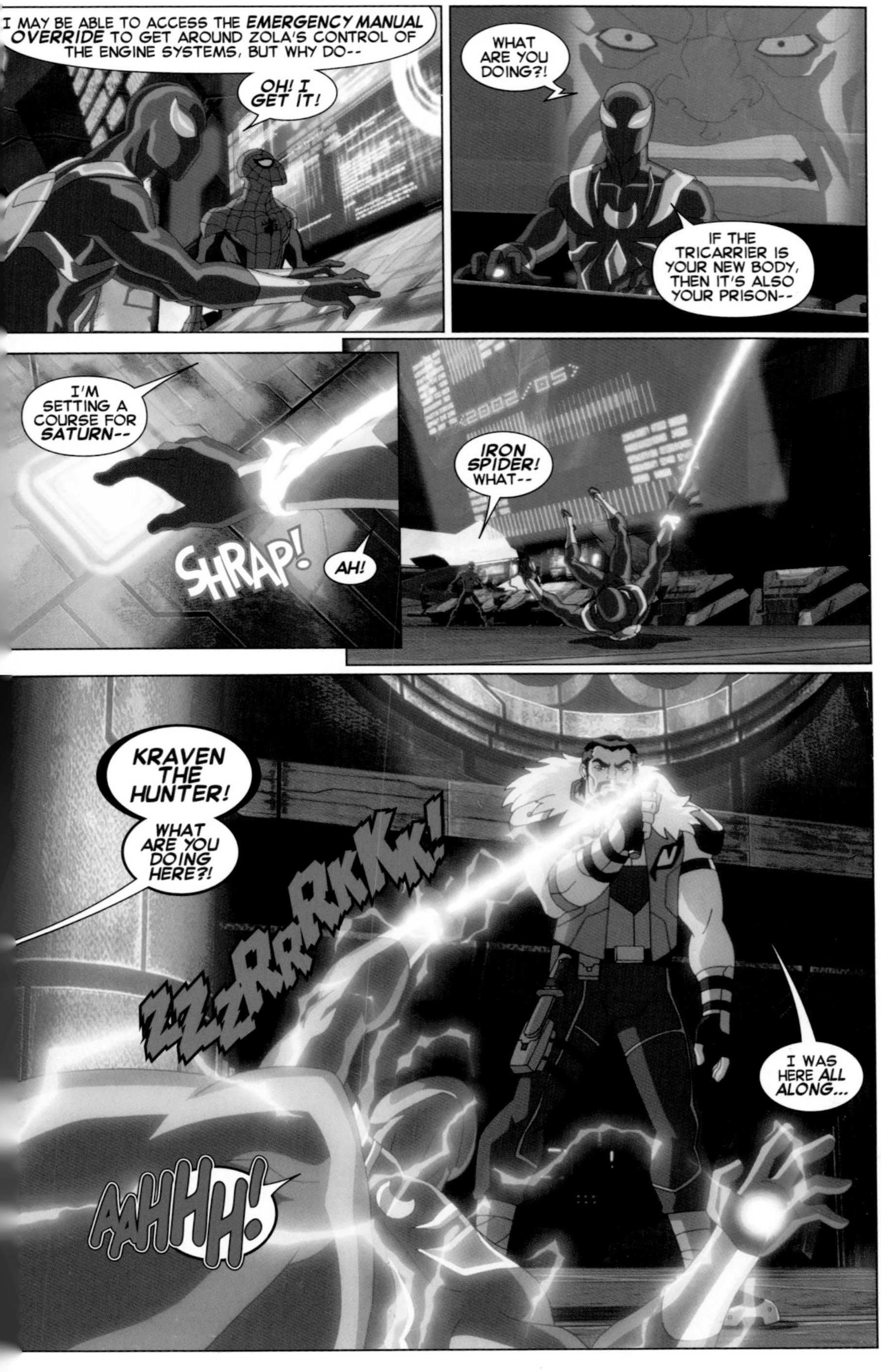

I MAY BE ABLE TO ACCESS THE EMERGENCY MANUAL OVERRIDE TO GET AROUND ZOLA'S CONTROL OF THE ENGINE SYSTEMS, BUT WHY DO--
OH! I GET IT!
WHAT ARE YOU DOING?!
IF THE TRICARRIER IS YOUR NEW BODY, THEN IT'S ALSO YOUR PRISON--
I'M SETTING A COURSE FOR SATURN--
SHRAP!
AH!
IRON SPIDER! WHAT--
KRAVEN THE HUNTER!
WHAT ARE YOU DOING HERE?!
ZZZRRRRKKK!
I WAS HERE ALL ALONG...
AAHHH!

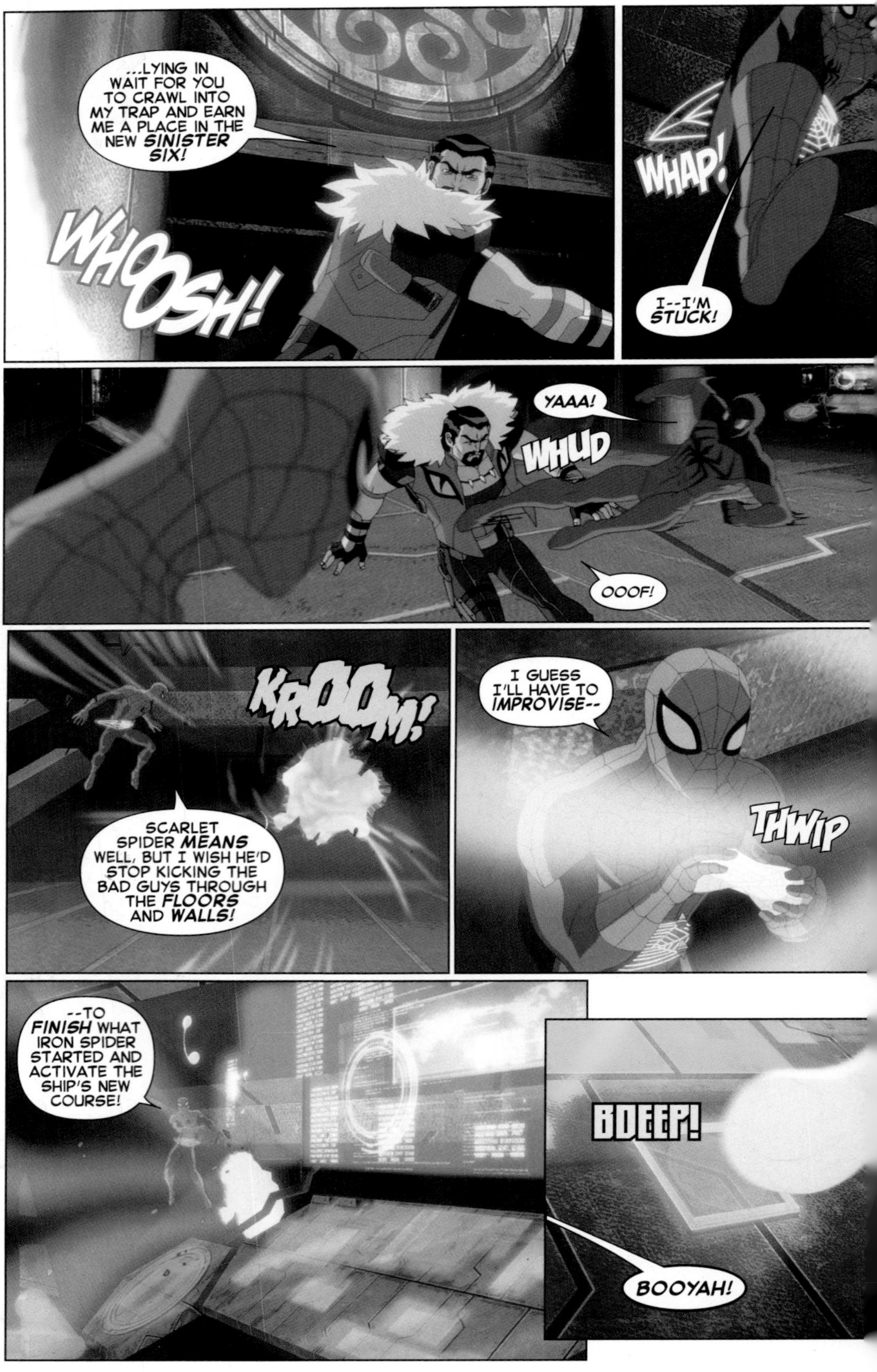
...LYING IN WAIT FOR YOU TO CRAWL INTO MY TRAP AND EARN ME A PLACE IN THE NEW SINISTER SIX!
WHOOSH!
WHAP!
I--I'M STUCK!
YAAA!
WHUD
OOOF!
KROOM!
SCARLET SPIDER MEANS WELL, BUT I WISH HE'D STOP KICKING THE BAD GUYS THROUGH THE FLOORS AND WALLS!
I GUESS I'LL HAVE TO IMPROVISE--
THWIP
--TO FINISH WHAT IRON SPIDER STARTED AND ACTIVATE THE SHIP'S NEW COURSE!
BDEEP!
BOOYAH!

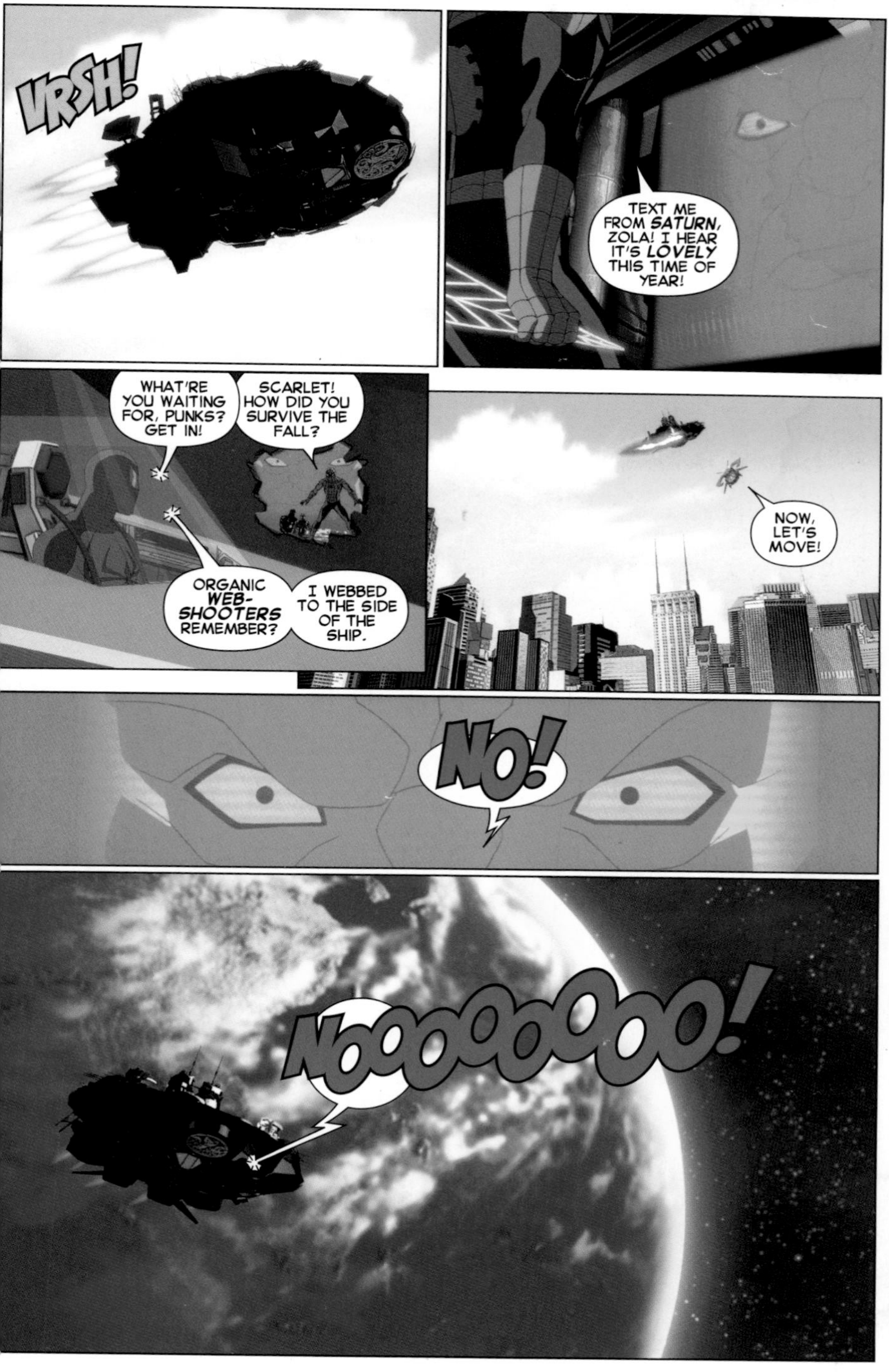
VRSH!
TEXT ME FROM SATURN, ZOLA! I HEAR IT'S LOVELY THIS TIME OF YEAR!
WHAT'RE YOU WAITING FOR, PUNKS? GET IN!
SCARLET! HOW DID YOU SURVIVE THE FALL?
ORGANIC WEB-SHOOTERS REMEMBER?
I WEBBED TO THE SIDE OF THE SHIP.
NOW, LET'S MOVE!
NO!
NOOOOOOOOO!

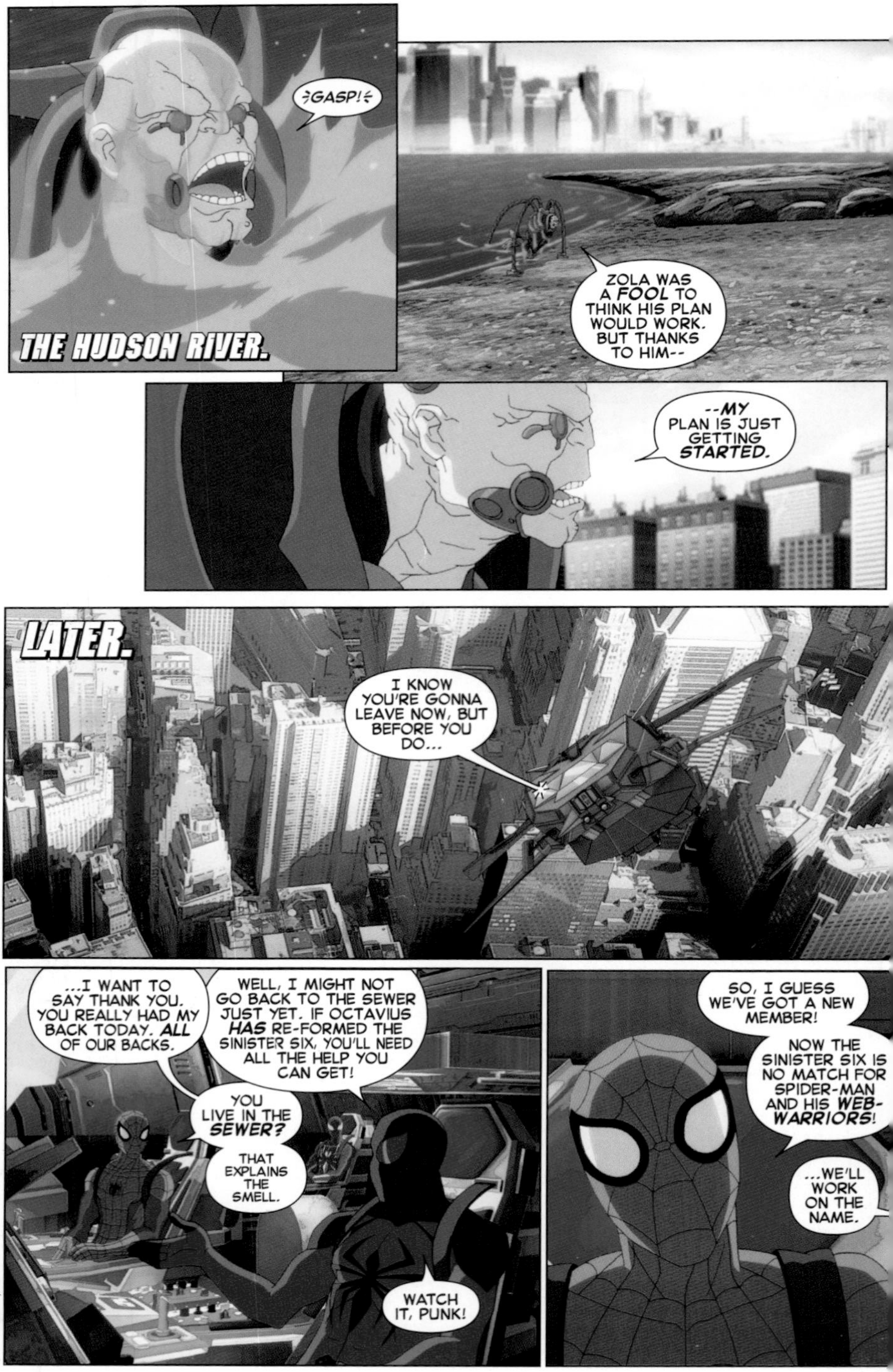

THE HUDSON RIVER.
GASP!
ZOLA WAS A FOOL TO THINK HIS PLAN WOULD WORK. BUT THANKS TO HIM--
--MY PLAN IS JUST GETTING STARTED.
LATER.
I KNOW YOU'RE GONNA LEAVE NOW, BUT BEFORE YOU DO...
...I WANT TO SAY THANK YOU. YOU REALLY HAD MY BACK TODAY. ALL OF OUR BACKS.
WELL, I MIGHT NOT GO BACK TO THE SEWER JUST YET. IF OCTAVIUS HAS RE-FORMED THE SINISTER SIX, YOU'LL NEED ALL THE HELP YOU CAN GET!
YOU LIVE IN THE SEWER?
THAT EXPLAINS THE SMELL.
WATCH IT, PUNK!
SO, I GUESS WE'VE GOT A NEW MEMBER!
NOW THE SINISTER SIX IS NO MATCH FOR SPIDER-MAN AND HIS WEB-WARRIORS!
...WE'LL WORK ON THE NAME.

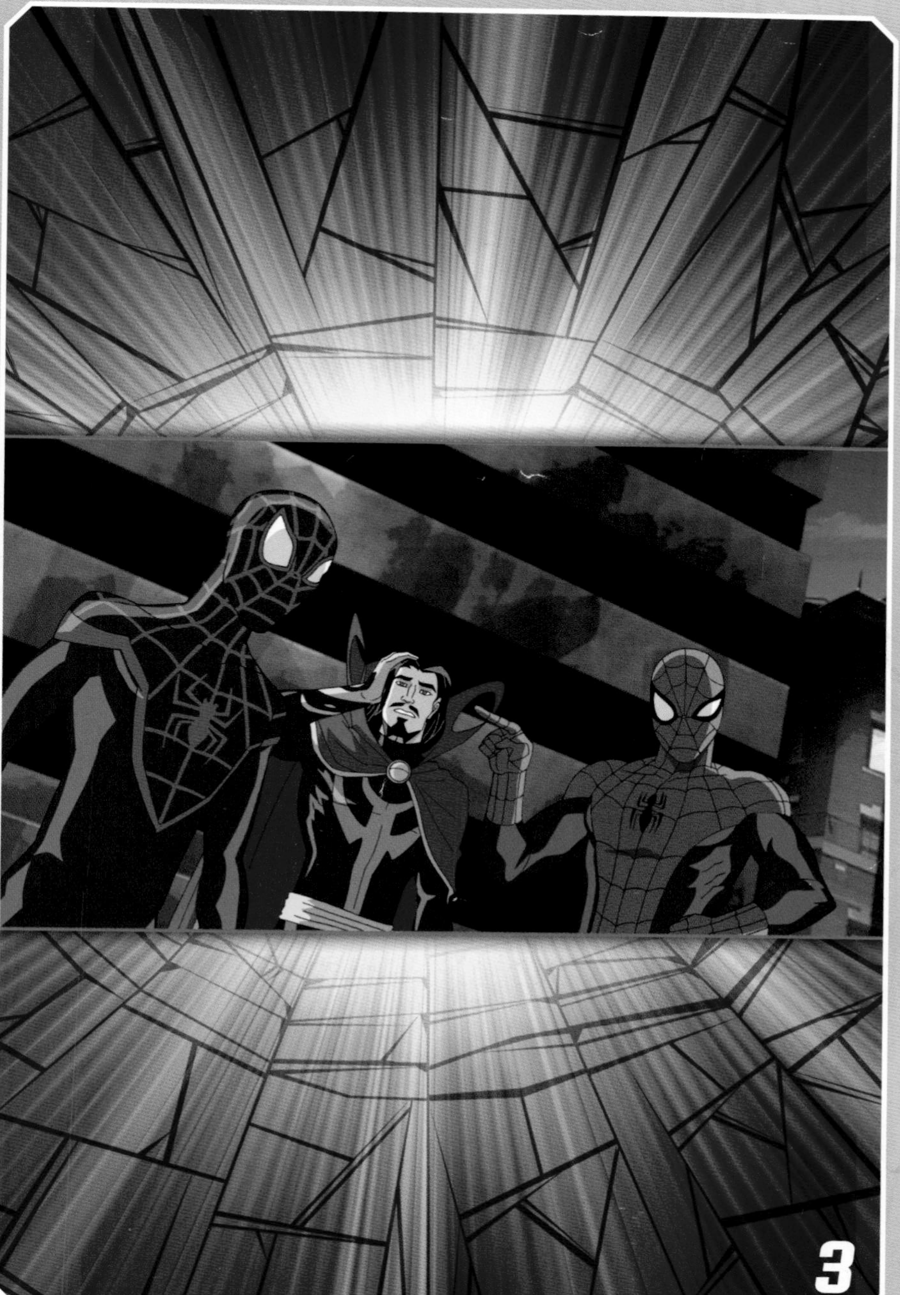

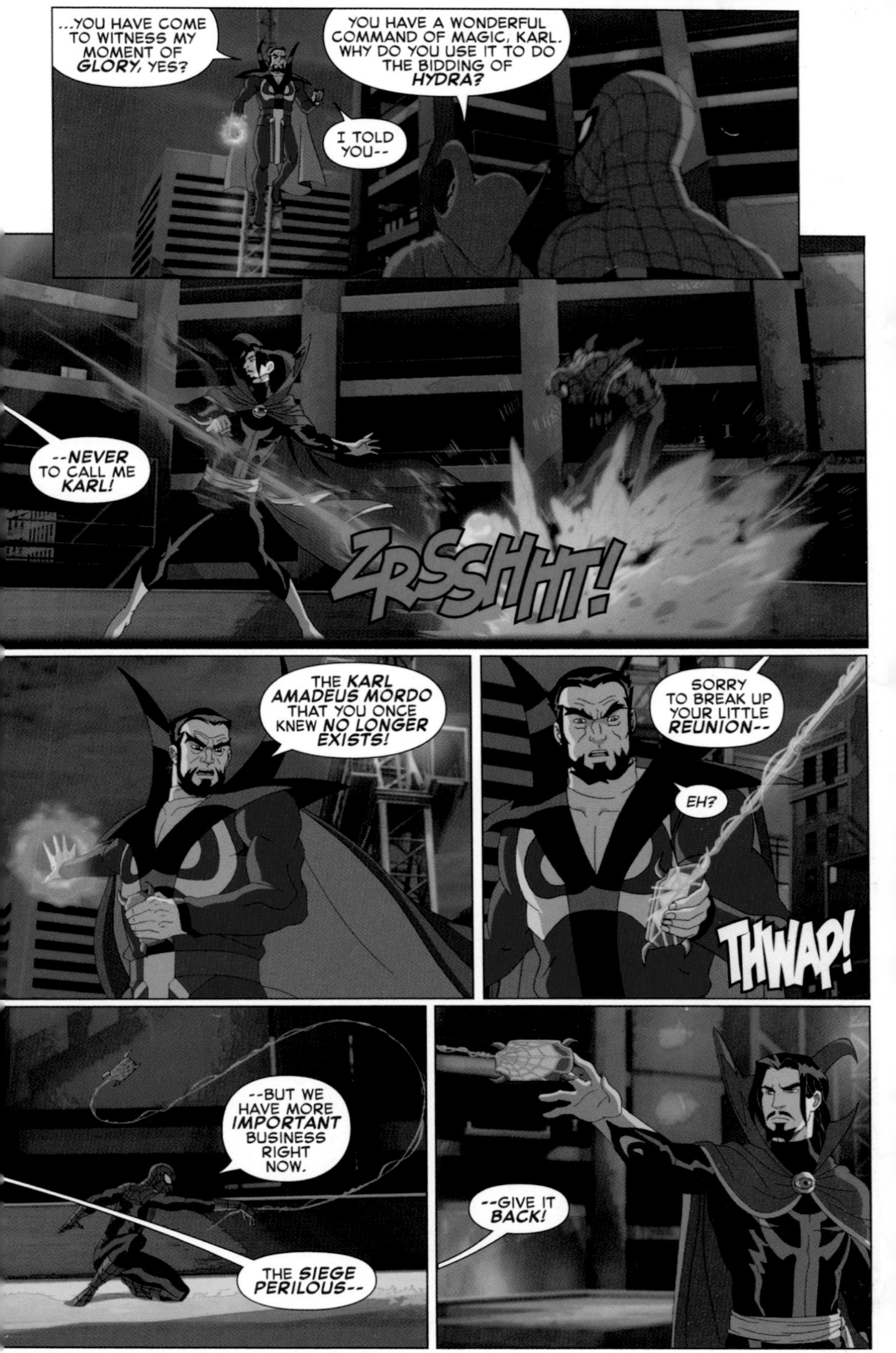
...YOU HAVE COME TO WITNESS MY MOMENT OF GLORY, YES?
YOU HAVE A WONDERFUL COMMAND OF MAGIC, KARL. WHY DO YOU USE IT TO DO THE BIDDING OF HYDRA?
I TOLD YOU--
--NEVER TO CALL ME KARL!
ZRSSHHT!
THE KARL AMADEUS MORDO THAT YOU ONCE KNEW NO LONGER EXISTS!
SORRY TO BREAK UP YOUR LITTLE REUNION--
EH?
THWAP!
--BUT WE HAVE MORE IMPORTANT BUSINESS RIGHT NOW.
THE SIEGE PERILOUS--
--GIVE IT BACK!

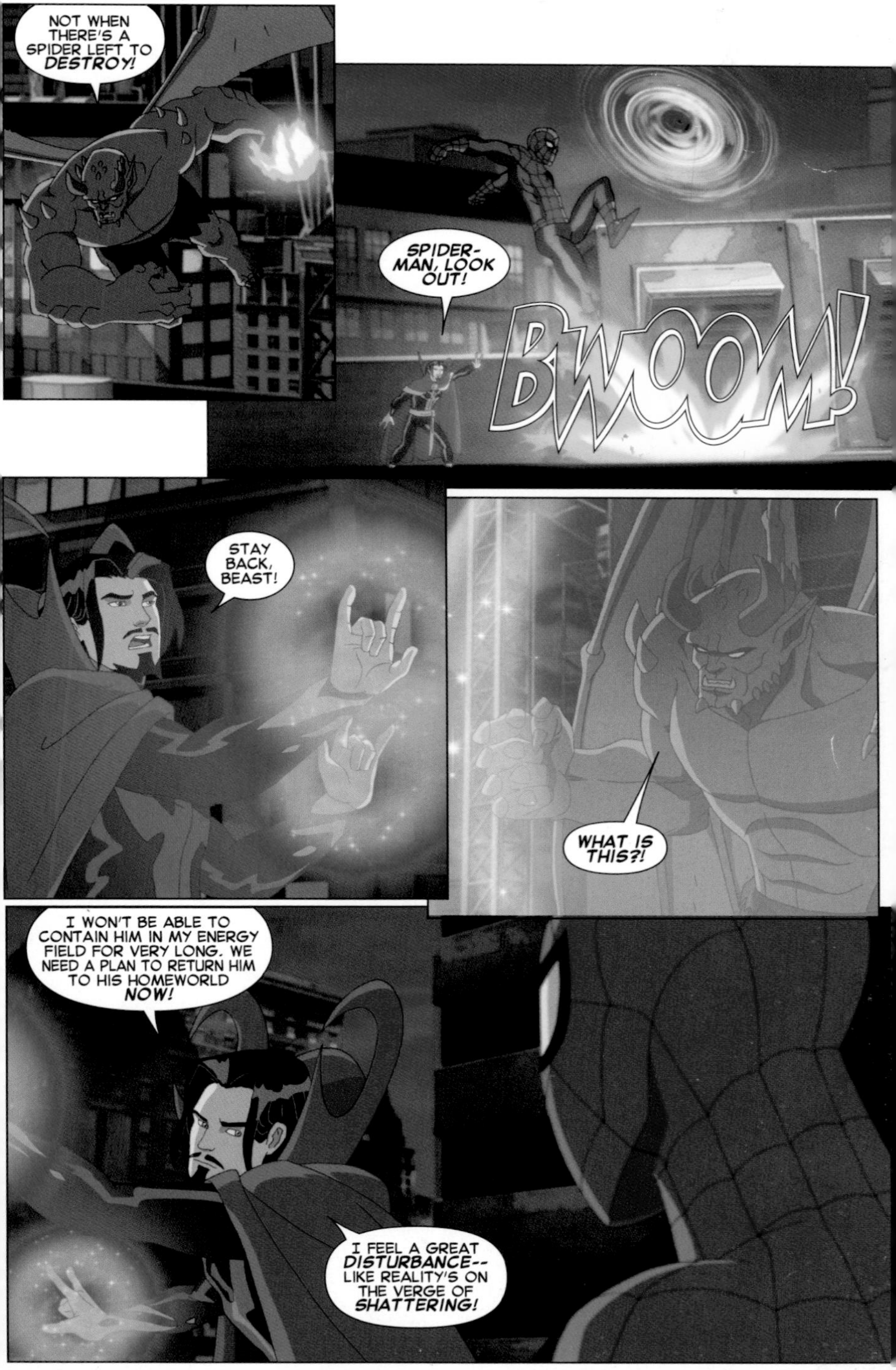
NOT WHEN THERE'S A SPIDER LEFT TO DESTROY!
SPIDER-MAN, LOOK OUT!
BWOOM!
STAY BACK, BEAST!
WHAT IS THIS?!
I WON'T BE ABLE TO CONTAIN HIM IN MY ENERGY FIELD FOR VERY LONG. WE NEED A PLAN TO RETURN HIM TO HIS HOMEWORLD NOW!
I FEEL A GREAT DISTURBANCE-- LIKE REALITY'S ON THE VERGE OF SHATTERING!

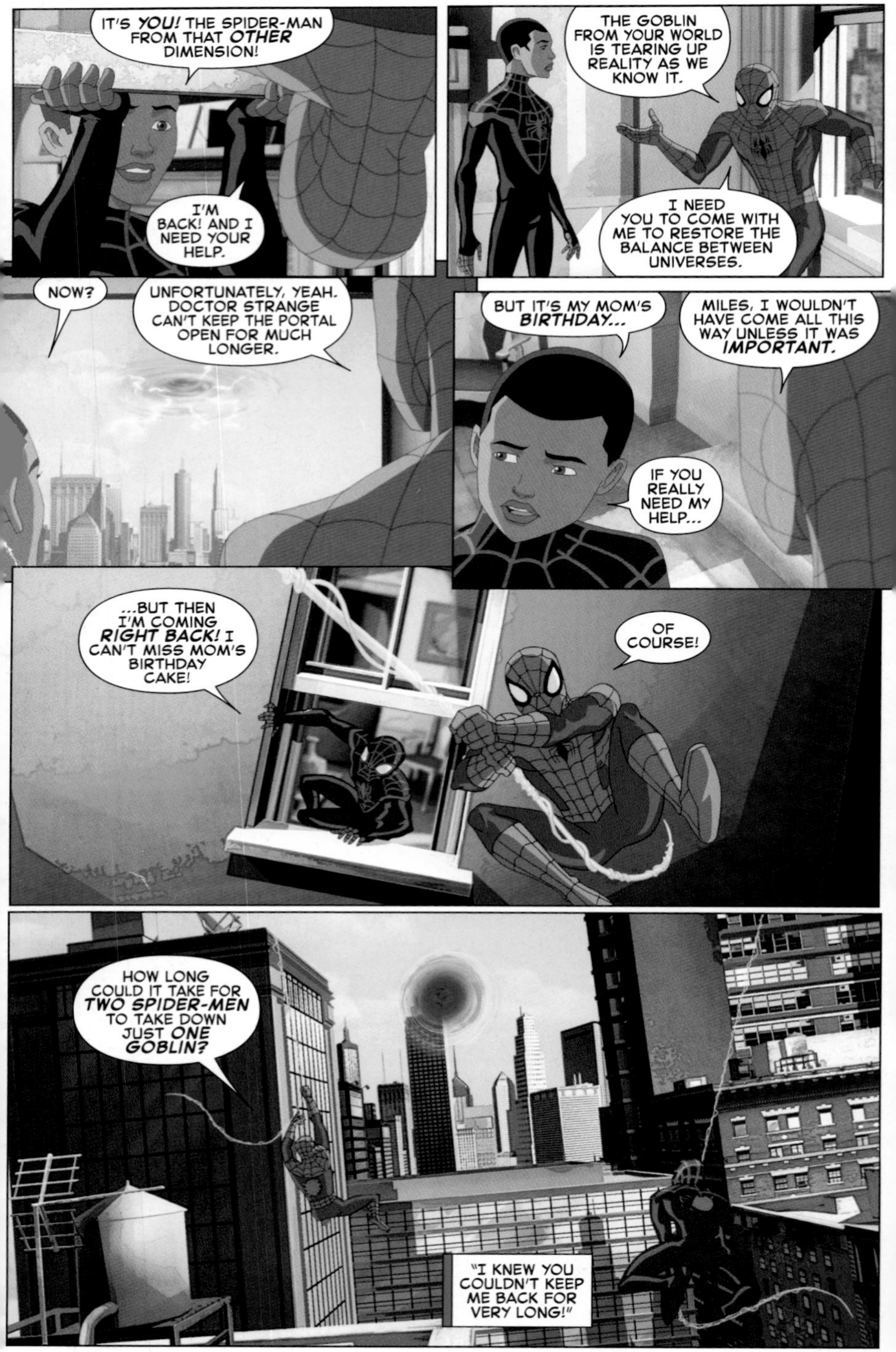
IT'S *YOU!* THE SPIDER-MAN FROM THAT *OTHER* DIMENSION!
I'M BACK! AND I NEED YOUR HELP.
THE GOBLIN FROM YOUR WORLD IS TEARING UP REALITY AS WE KNOW IT.
I NEED YOU TO COME WITH ME TO RESTORE THE BALANCE BETWEEN UNIVERSES.
NOW?
UNFORTUNATELY, YEAH. DOCTOR STRANGE CAN'T KEEP THE PORTAL OPEN FOR MUCH LONGER.
BUT IT'S MY MOM'S *BIRTHDAY...*
MILES, I WOULDN'T HAVE COME ALL THIS WAY UNLESS IT WAS *IMPORTANT.*
IF YOU REALLY NEED MY HELP...
...BUT THEN I'M COMING *RIGHT BACK!* I CAN'T MISS MOM'S BIRTHDAY CAKE!
OF COURSE!
HOW LONG COULD IT TAKE FOR *TWO SPIDER-MEN* TO TAKE DOWN JUST *ONE GOBLIN?*
"I KNEW YOU COULDN'T KEEP ME BACK FOR VERY LONG!"

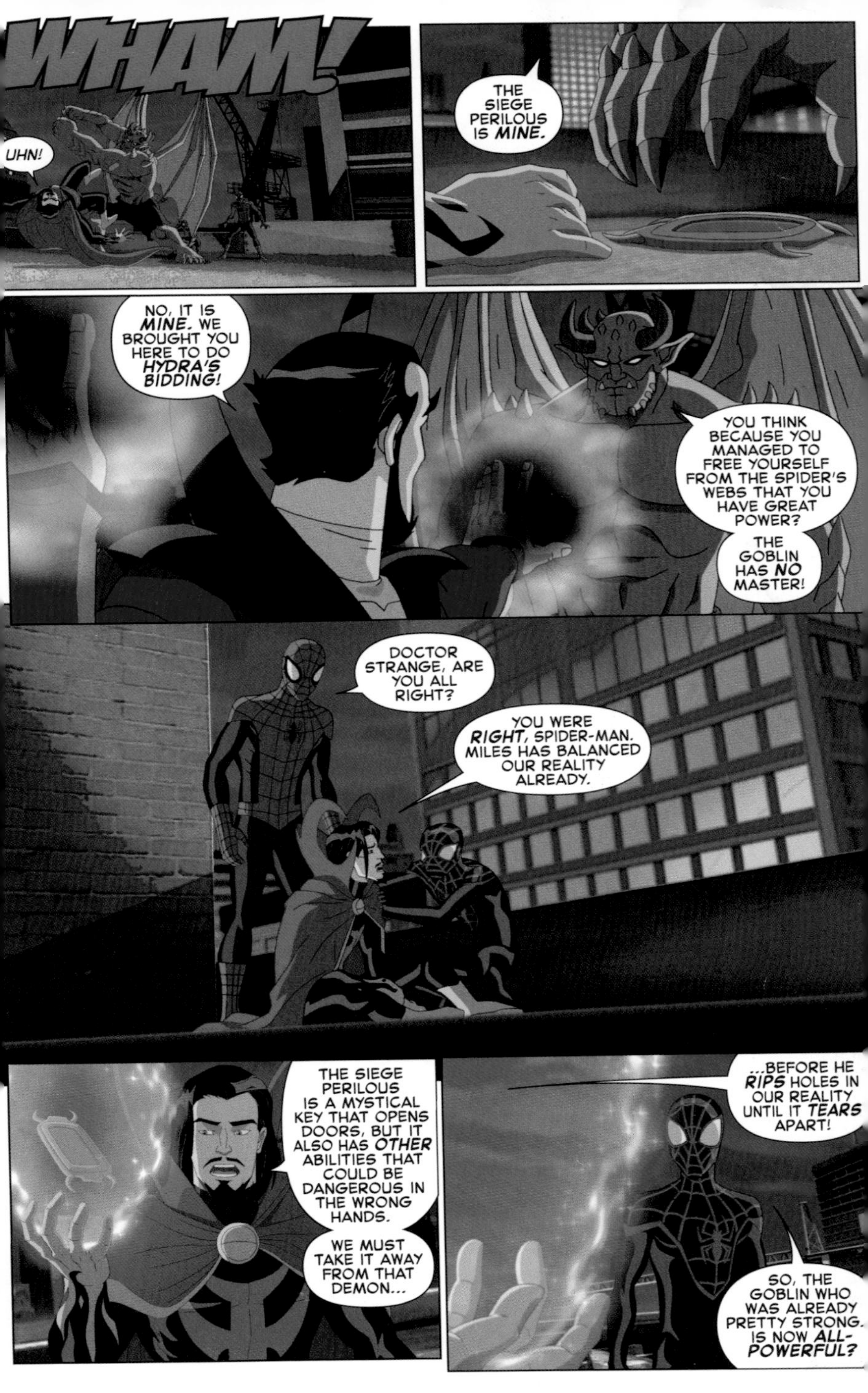
WHAM!
UHN!
THE SIEGE PERILOUS IS MINE.
NO, IT IS MINE. WE BROUGHT YOU HERE TO DO HYDRA'S BIDDING!
YOU THINK BECAUSE YOU MANAGED TO FREE YOURSELF FROM THE SPIDER'S WEBS THAT YOU HAVE GREAT POWER?
THE GOBLIN HAS NO MASTER!
DOCTOR STRANGE, ARE YOU ALL RIGHT?
YOU WERE RIGHT, SPIDER-MAN. MILES HAS BALANCED OUR REALITY ALREADY.
THE SIEGE PERILOUS IS A MYSTICAL KEY THAT OPENS DOORS, BUT IT ALSO HAS OTHER ABILITIES THAT COULD BE DANGEROUS IN THE WRONG HANDS.
WE MUST TAKE IT AWAY FROM THAT DEMON...
...BEFORE HE RIPS HOLES IN OUR REALITY UNTIL IT TEARS APART!
SO, THE GOBLIN WHO WAS ALREADY PRETTY STRONG, IS NOW ALL-POWERFUL?

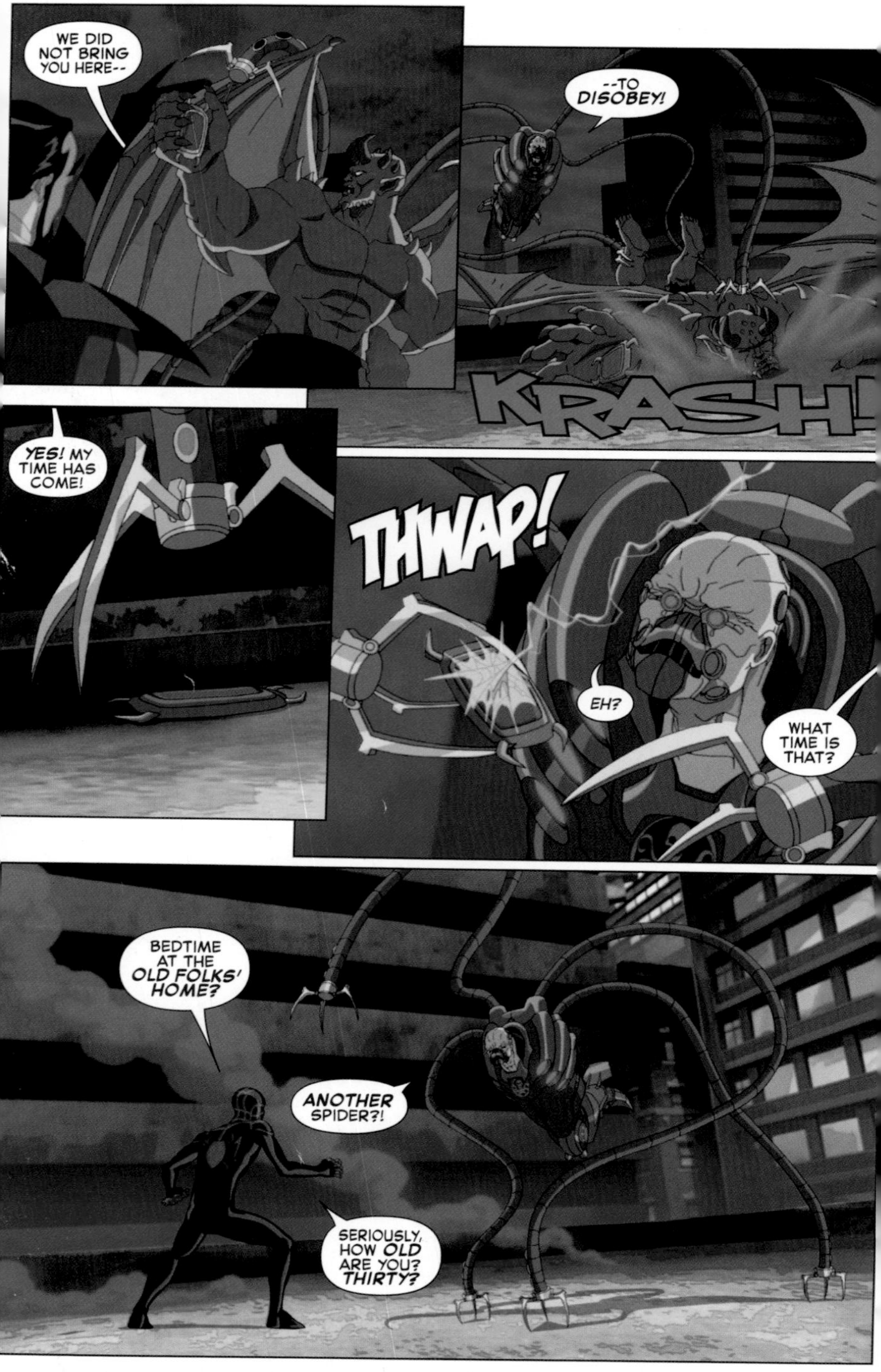
WE DID NOT BRING YOU HERE--
--TO DISOBEY!
KRASH!
YES! MY TIME HAS COME!
THWAP!
EH?
WHAT TIME IS THAT?
BEDTIME AT THE OLD FOLKS' HOME?
ANOTHER SPIDER?!
SERIOUSLY, HOW OLD ARE YOU? THIRTY?

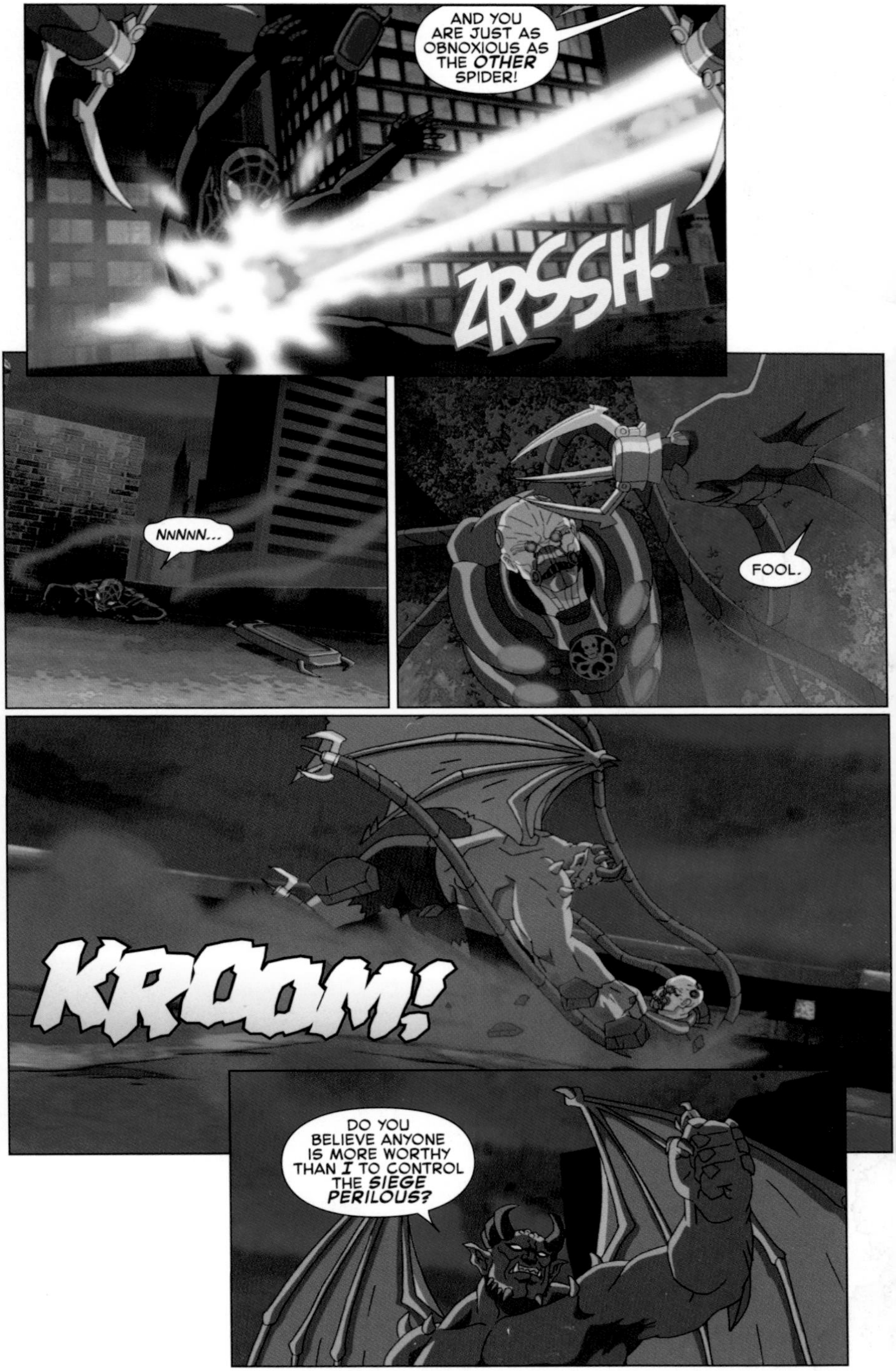
AND YOU ARE JUST AS OBNOXIOUS AS THE OTHER SPIDER!
ZRSSH!
NNNNN...
FOOL.
KROOM!
DO YOU BELIEVE ANYONE IS MORE WORTHY THAN I TO CONTROL THE SIEGE PERILOUS?

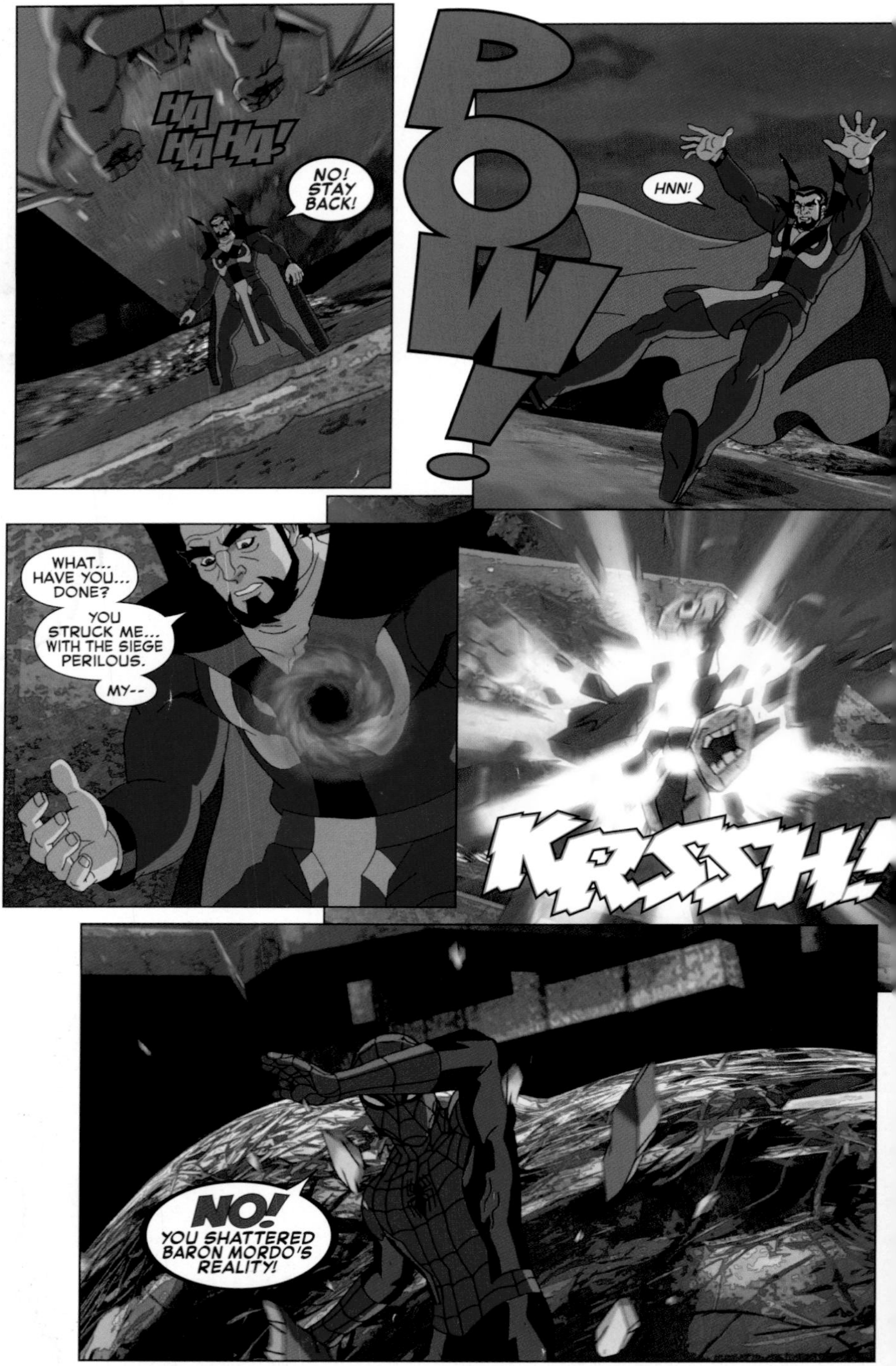
HA HA HA HA!
NO! STAY BACK!
POW!
HNN!
WHAT... HAVE YOU... DONE?
YOU STRUCK ME... WITH THE SIEGE PERILOUS.
MY--
KRSSH!
NO! YOU SHATTERED BARON MORDO'S REALITY!

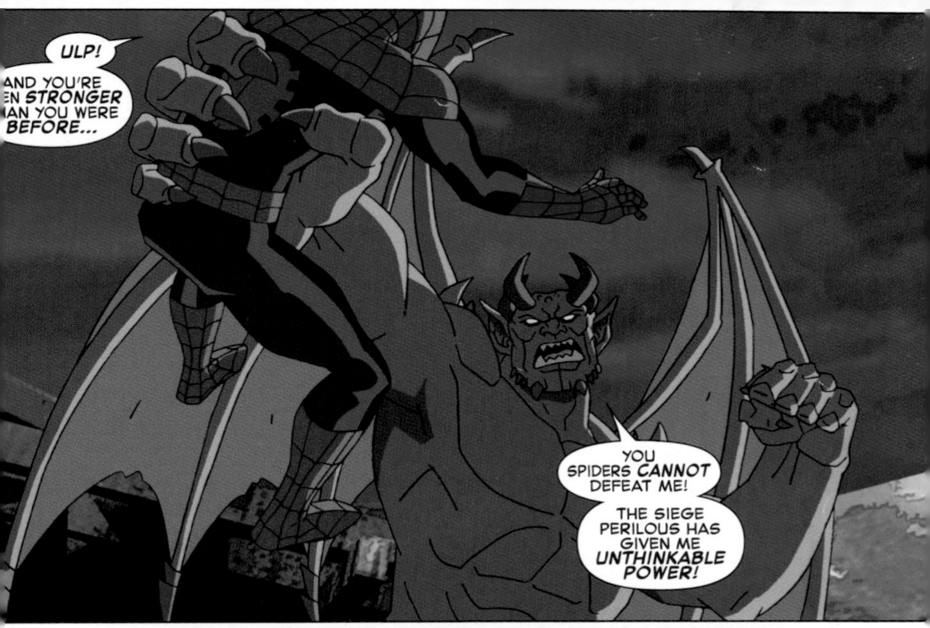
ULP!
AND YOU'RE EN STRONGER AN YOU WERE BEFORE...
YOU SPIDERS CANNOT DEFEAT ME!
THE SIEGE PERILOUS HAS GIVEN ME UNTHINKABLE POWER!

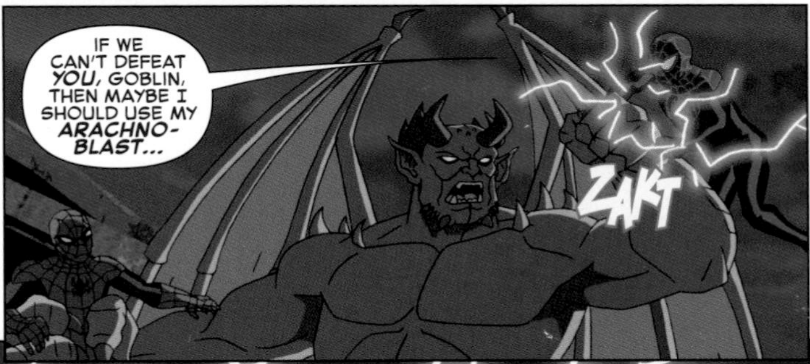
IF WE CAN'T DEFEAT YOU, GOBLIN, THEN MAYBE I SHOULD USE MY ARACHNO-BLAST...
ZAKT

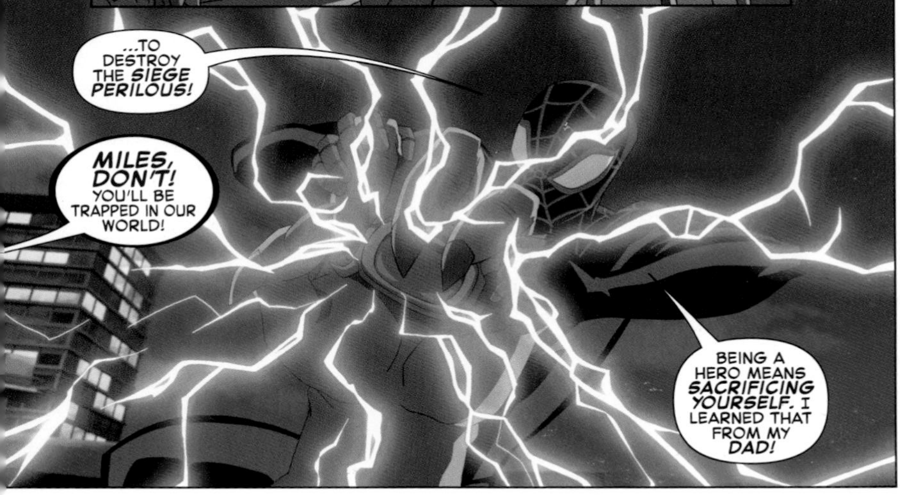
...TO DESTROY THE SIEGE PERILOUS!
MILES, DON'T! YOU'LL BE TRAPPED IN OUR WORLD!
BEING A HERO MEANS SACRIFICING YOURSELF. I LEARNED THAT FROM MY DAD!

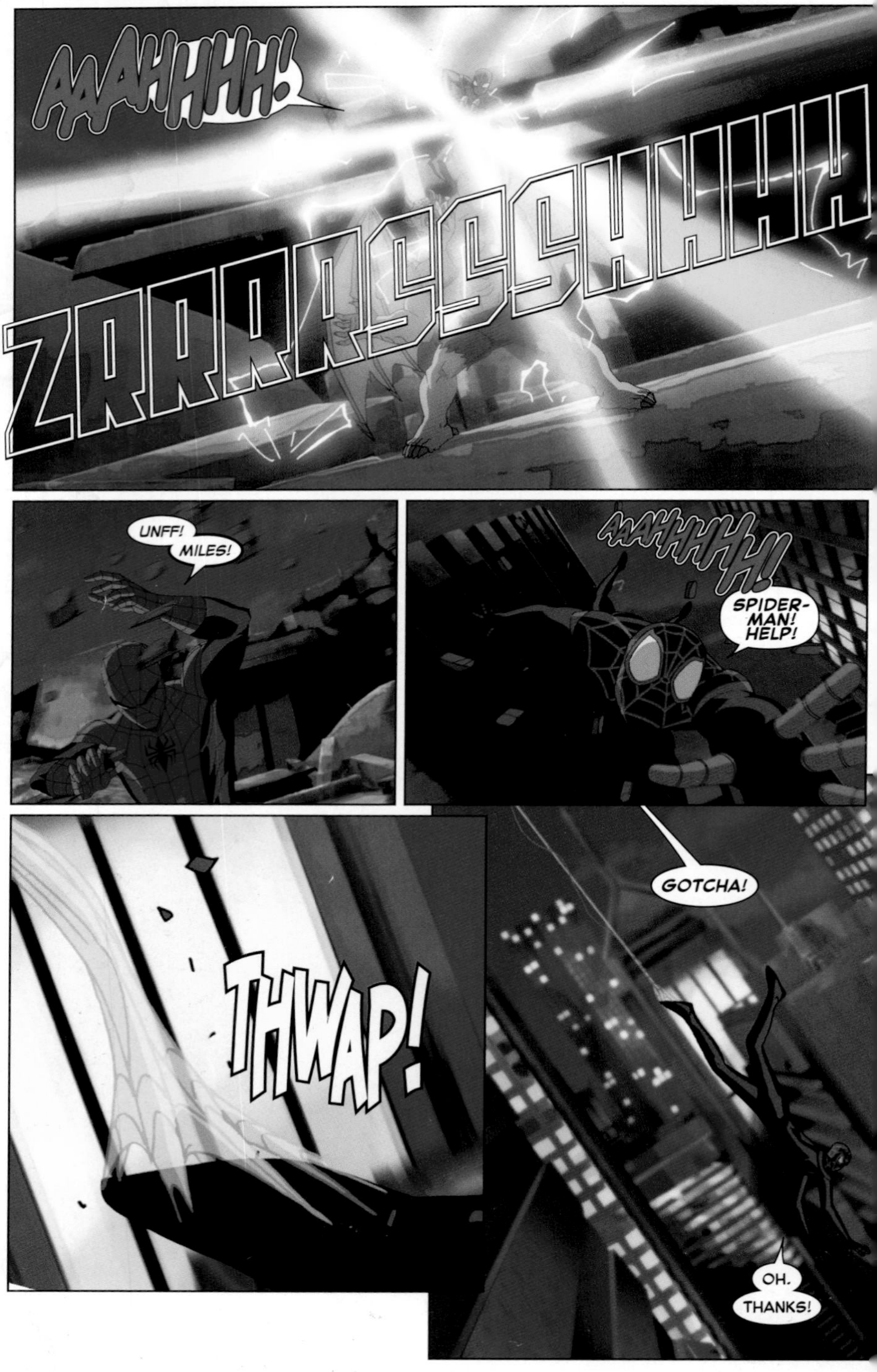
AAAHHHH!
ZRRRASSSCHHHHH
UNFF! MILES!
AAAHHHHH!
SPIDER-MAN! HELP!
THWAP!
GOTCHA!
OH. THANKS!

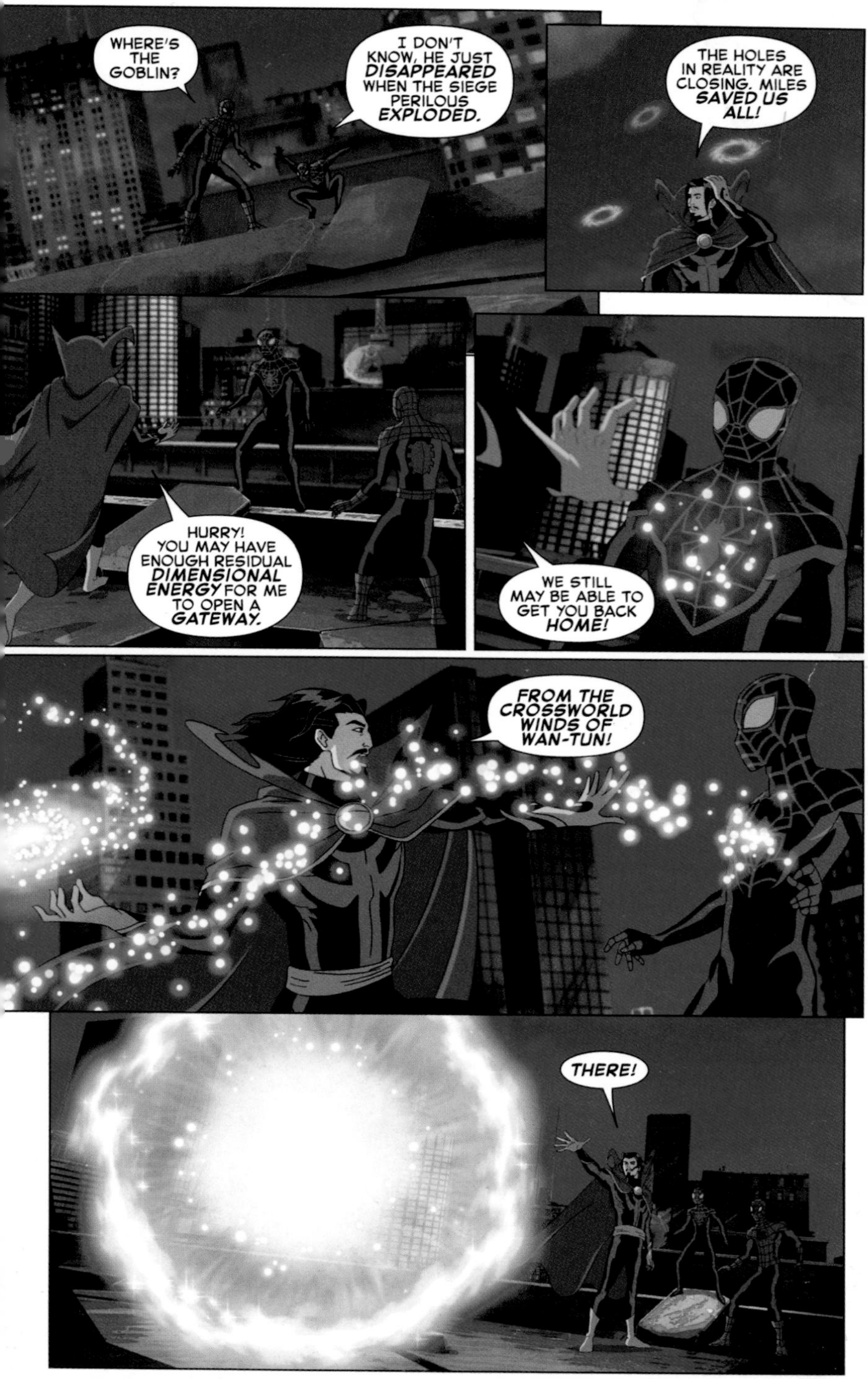
WHERE'S THE GOBLIN?
I DON'T KNOW, HE JUST DISAPPEARED WHEN THE SIEGE PERILOUS EXPLODED.
THE HOLES IN REALITY ARE CLOSING. MILES SAVED US ALL!
HURRY! YOU MAY HAVE ENOUGH RESIDUAL DIMENSIONAL ENERGY FOR ME TO OPEN A GATEWAY.
WE STILL MAY BE ABLE TO GET YOU BACK HOME!
FROM THE CROSSWORLD WINDS OF WAN-TUN!
THERE!

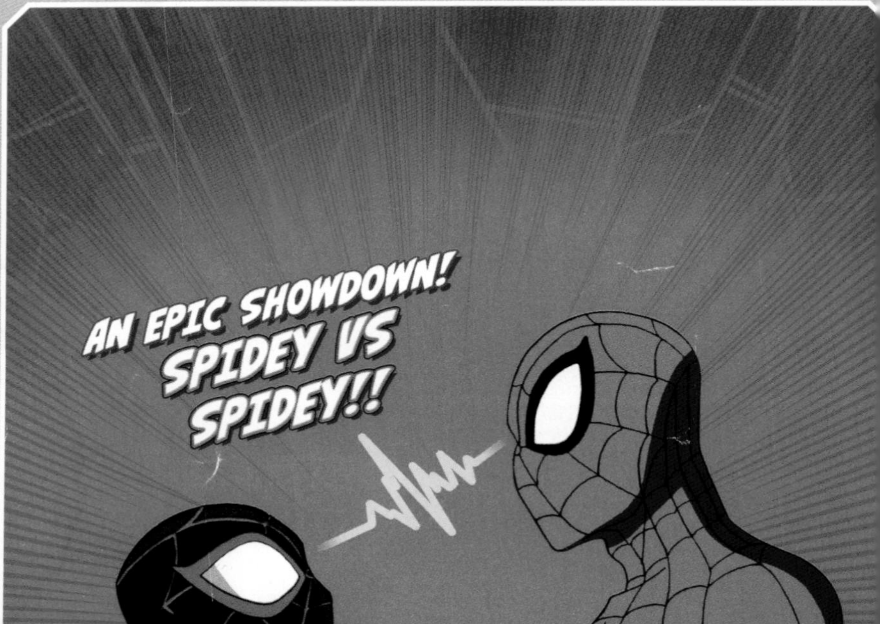
AN EPIC SHOWDOWN! SPIDEY VS SPIDEY!!

"--HARRY OSBORN'S THE *COOLEST*."

THIS IS AWESOME! I DIDN'T KNOW THIS GAME HAD *BATTLE MODE!*

ALL GAMES HAVE BATTLE MODE!

BATTLING IS *FUN!*

WELL, NOT ALWAYS.

CONGRATULATIONS, MILES!

I WON? *I WON!*

ANYONE WHO CAN BEAT ME IN *SNOWBOARD RACER XL SUPREME* IS OKAY IN MY BOOK! WHERE HAVE YOU BEEN *HIDING* THIS MILES KID, PETEY?

SON? ARE YOU HOME? I DECIDED TO COME BACK A DAY *EARLY!*

DAD!

HI, NORMAN!

N-NORMAN?

NORMAN OSBORN?!

PETER, THAT DUDE'S THE *GOBLIN!*

THAT DUDE *WAS* THE GOBLIN. NORMAN'S *CURED* NOW.

PETER! IT'S GOOD TO SEE YOU AGAIN.

HARRY SAYS YOUR FRIEND HERE JUST BEAT HIM DOWN THE SLOPE.

THIS IS *MILES MORALES.*

WELL, MILES, TODAY MIGHT BE YOUR *UNLUCKY DAY.* HARRY'S GOOD, BUT *I'M* STILL THE SNOWBOARD CHAMP IN THIS HOUSE.

CARE TO CHALLENGE ME FOR THE TITLE?

BOOOOM!

HARRY, GET DOWN!

WHAT WAS--?

SKREEEEEE!

IT'S THE *VULTURE!*

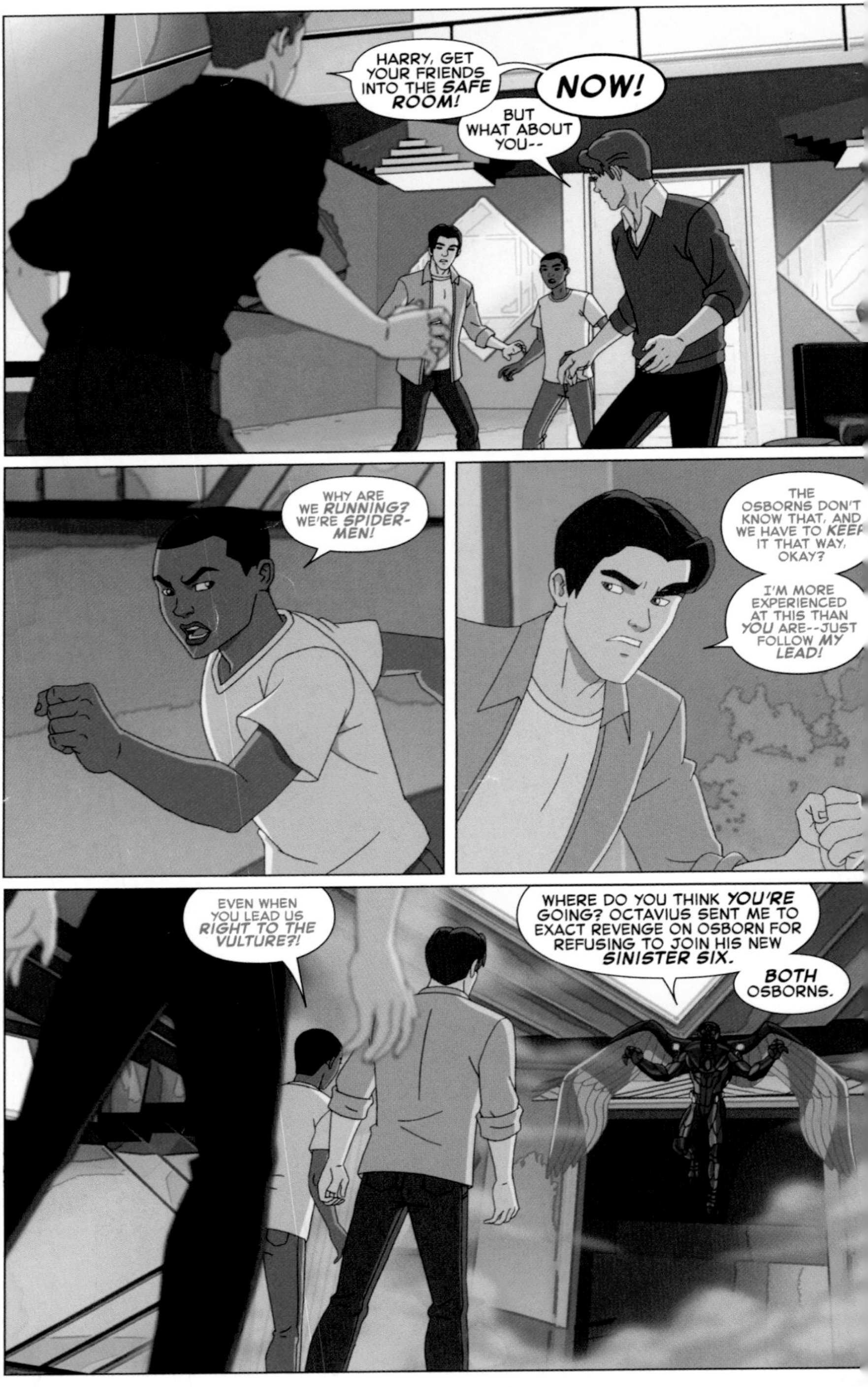
HARRY, GET YOUR FRIENDS INTO THE SAFE ROOM!
NOW!
BUT WHAT ABOUT YOU--
WHY ARE WE RUNNING? WE'RE SPIDER-MEN!
THE OSBORNS DON'T KNOW THAT, AND WE HAVE TO KEEP IT THAT WAY, OKAY?
I'M MORE EXPERIENCED AT THIS THAN YOU ARE--JUST FOLLOW MY LEAD!
EVEN WHEN YOU LEAD US RIGHT TO THE VULTURE?!
WHERE DO YOU THINK YOU'RE GOING? OCTAVIUS SENT ME TO EXACT REVENGE ON OSBORN FOR REFUSING TO JOIN HIS NEW SINISTER SIX.
BOTH OSBORNS.

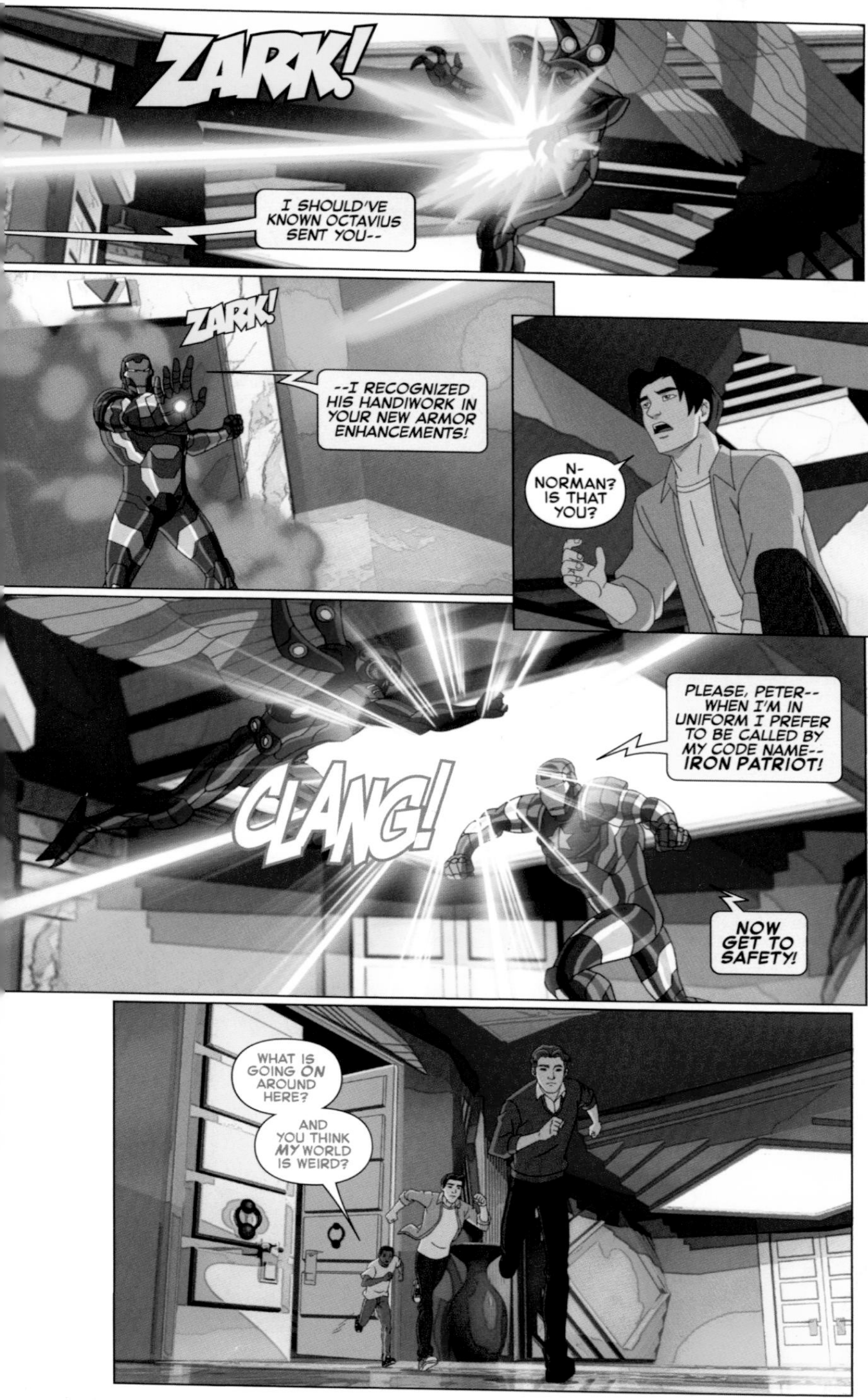
ZARK!
I SHOULD'VE KNOWN OCTAVIUS SENT YOU--
ZARK!
--I RECOGNIZED HIS HANDIWORK IN YOUR NEW ARMOR ENHANCEMENTS!
N-NORMAN? IS THAT YOU?
PLEASE, PETER--WHEN I'M IN UNIFORM I PREFER TO BE CALLED BY MY CODE NAME--IRON PATRIOT!
CLANG!
NOW GET TO SAFETY!
WHAT IS GOING ON AROUND HERE?
AND YOU THINK MY WORLD IS WEIRD?

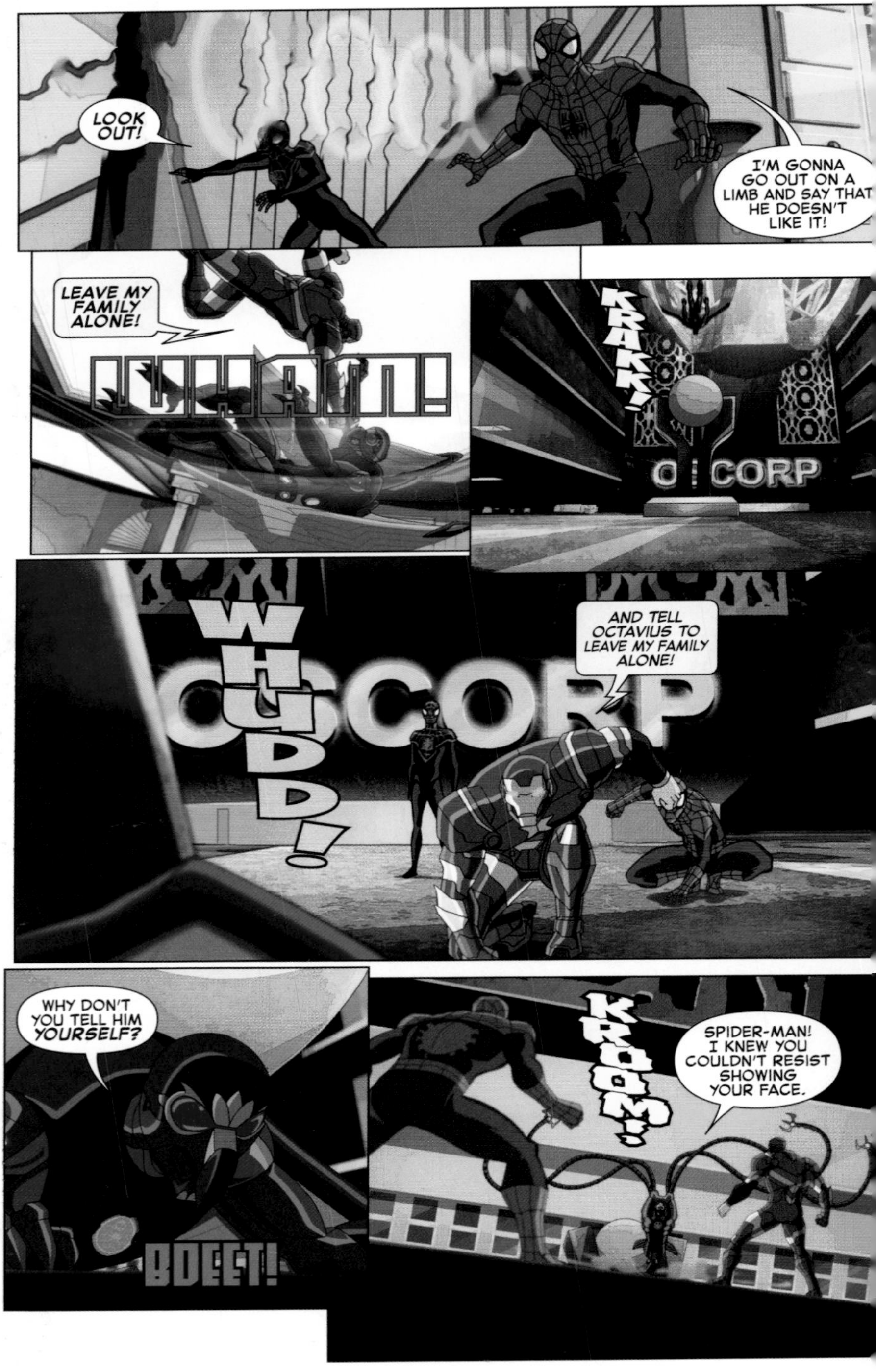
LOOK OUT!
I'M GONNA GO OUT ON A LIMB AND SAY THAT HE DOESN'T LIKE IT!
LEAVE MY FAMILY ALONE!
WHAAM!
KRAKK!
O CORP
AND TELL OCTAVIUS TO LEAVE MY FAMILY ALONE!
WHUDD!
OSCORP
WHY DON'T YOU TELL HIM YOURSELF?
BDEET!
KROOM!
SPIDER-MAN! I KNEW YOU COULDN'T RESIST SHOWING YOUR FACE.

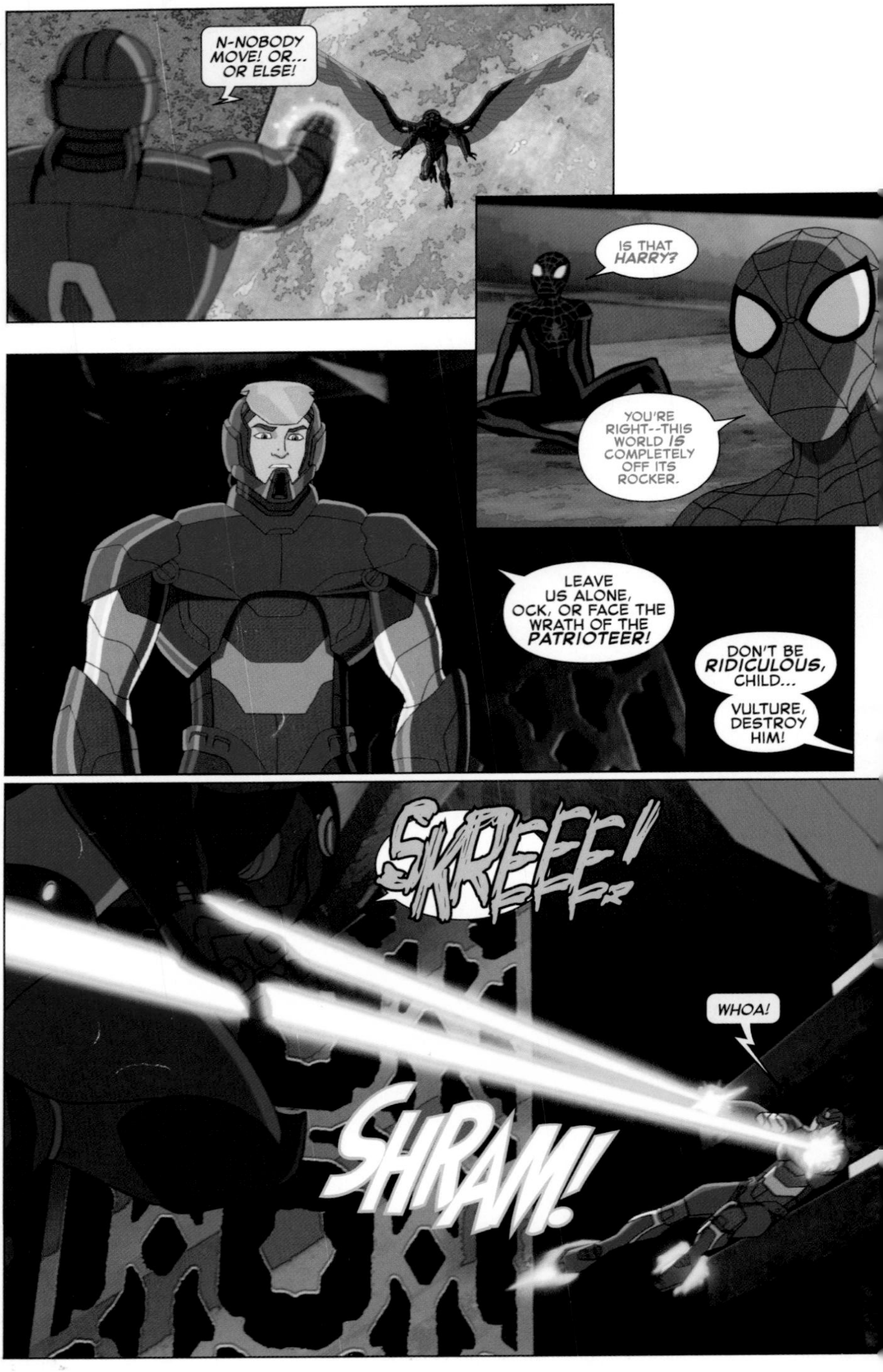
N-NOBODY MOVE! OR... OR ELSE!
IS THAT *HARRY?*
YOU'RE RIGHT--THIS WORLD *IS* COMPLETELY OFF ITS ROCKER.
LEAVE US ALONE, OCK, OR FACE THE WRATH OF THE *PATRIOTEER!*
DON'T BE *RIDICULOUS,* CHILD...
VULTURE, DESTROY HIM!
SKREEE!
WHOA!
SHRAM!

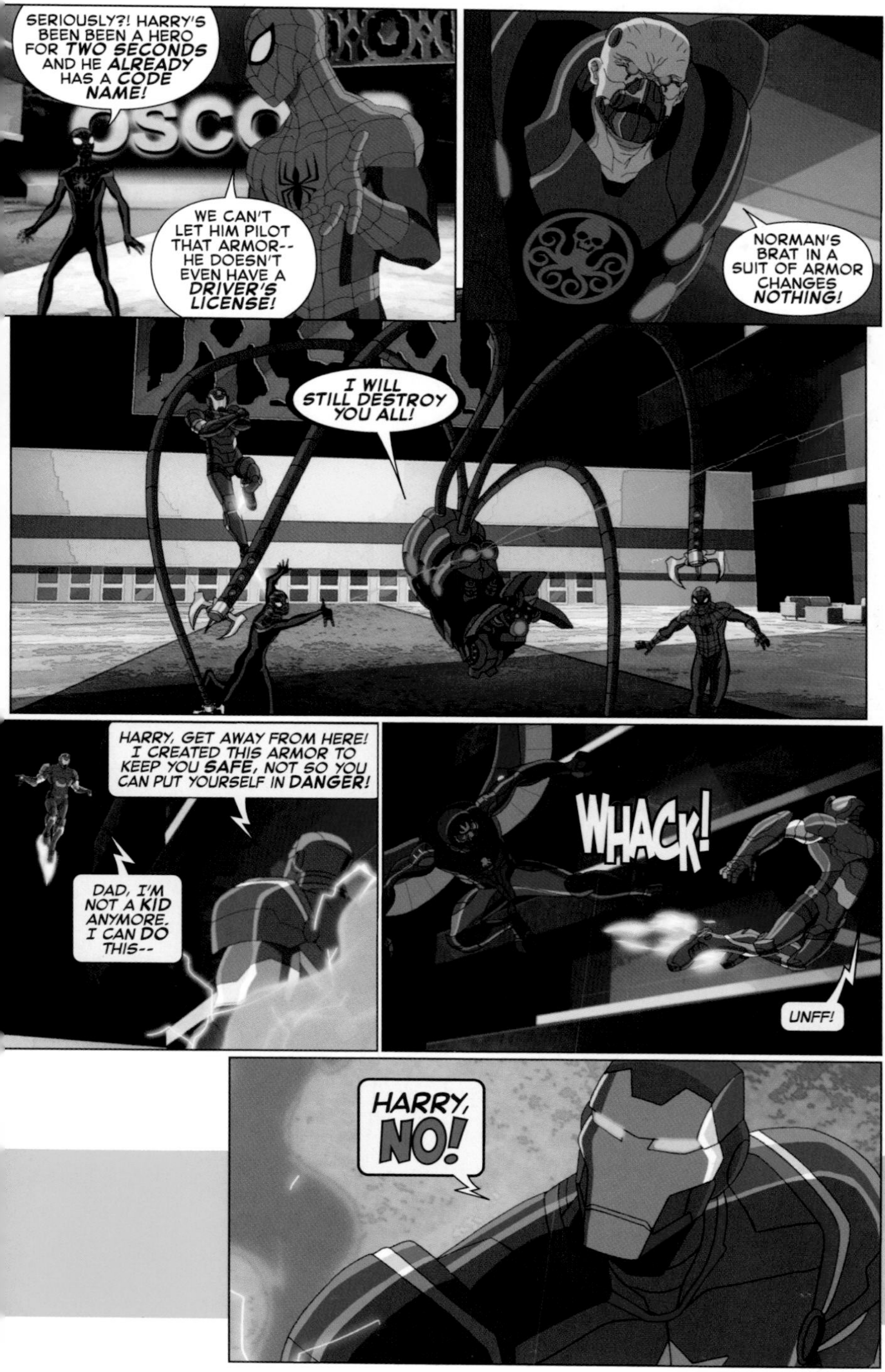
SERIOUSLY?! HARRY'S BEEN BEEN A HERO FOR TWO SECONDS AND HE ALREADY HAS A CODE NAME!
WE CAN'T LET HIM PILOT THAT ARMOR-- HE DOESN'T EVEN HAVE A DRIVER'S LICENSE!
OSCO
NORMAN'S BRAT IN A SUIT OF ARMOR CHANGES NOTHING!
I WILL STILL DESTROY YOU ALL!
HARRY, GET AWAY FROM HERE! I CREATED THIS ARMOR TO KEEP YOU SAFE, NOT SO YOU CAN PUT YOURSELF IN DANGER!
DAD, I'M NOT A KID ANYMORE. I CAN DO THIS--
WHACK!
UNFF!
HARRY, NO!

YOUR KID IS IN OVER HIS HEAD--JUST LIKE HIS FATHER!

CRNCH

NOW, WHERE WERE WE?

SKRAK!

OH, YEAH--

GAH!

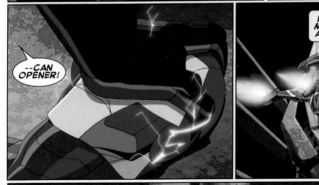

--CAN OPENER!

LEAVE MY DAD ALONE!

WHACK!

YES! KEEP IT UP, SON!

NORMAN, NO! WE HAVE TO KEEP HARRY SAFE!

MAYBE I WAS WRONG ABOUT HARRY, SPIDER-MAN. MAYBE HE CAN HANDLE HIMSELF.

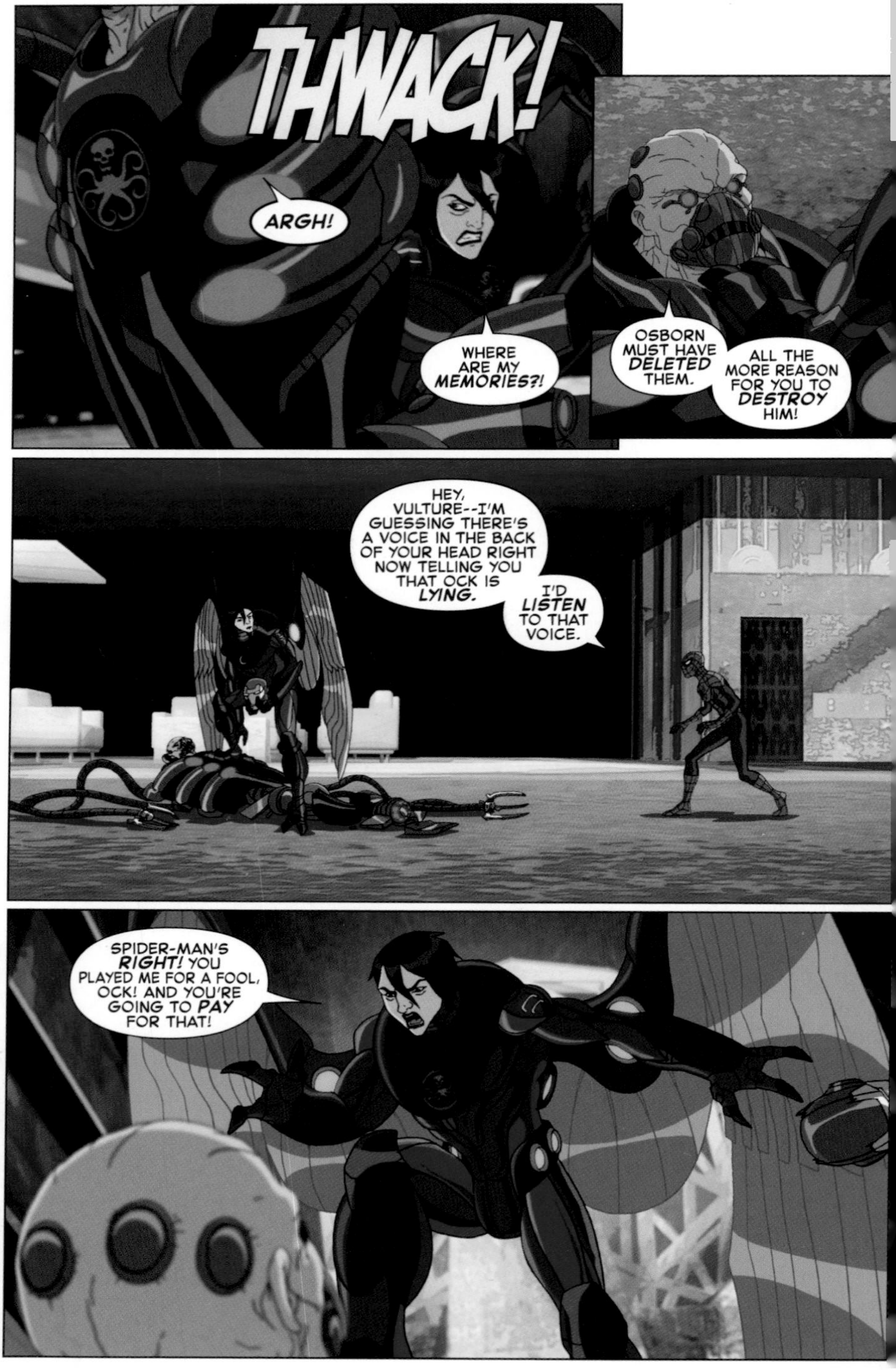
THWACK!
ARGH!
WHERE ARE MY MEMORIES?!
OSBORN MUST HAVE DELETED THEM.
ALL THE MORE REASON FOR YOU TO DESTROY HIM!
HEY, VULTURE--I'M GUESSING THERE'S A VOICE IN THE BACK OF YOUR HEAD RIGHT NOW TELLING YOU THAT OCK IS LYING.
I'D LISTEN TO THAT VOICE.
SPIDER-MAN'S RIGHT! YOU PLAYED ME FOR A FOOL, OCK! AND YOU'RE GOING TO PAY FOR THAT!

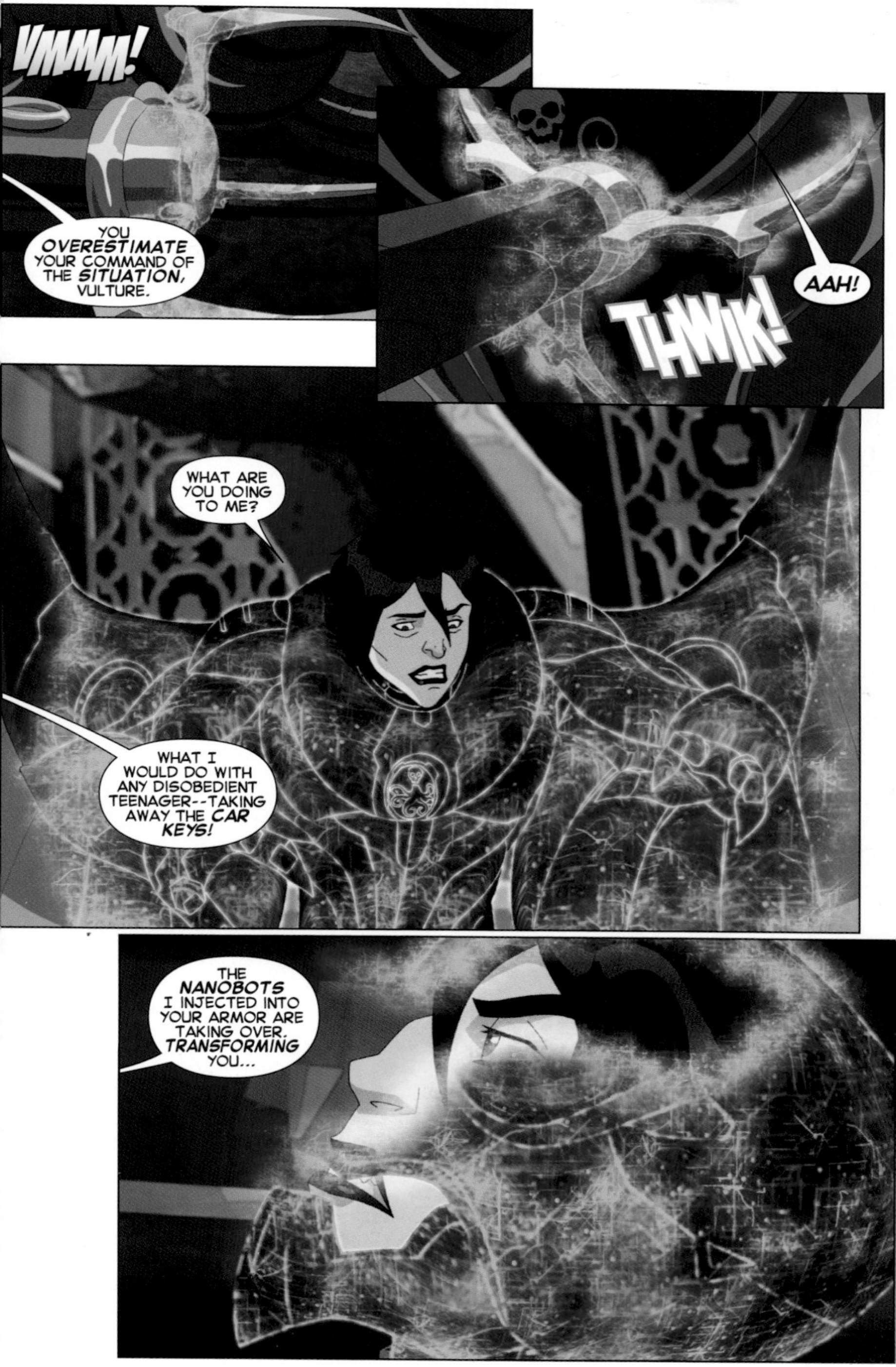
VMMM!
YOU OVERESTIMATE YOUR COMMAND OF THE SITUATION, VULTURE.
THWIK!
AAH!
WHAT ARE YOU DOING TO ME?
WHAT I WOULD DO WITH ANY DISOBEDIENT TEENAGER--TAKING AWAY THE CAR KEYS!
THE NANOBOTS I INJECTED INTO YOUR ARMOR ARE TAKING OVER. TRANSFORMING YOU...

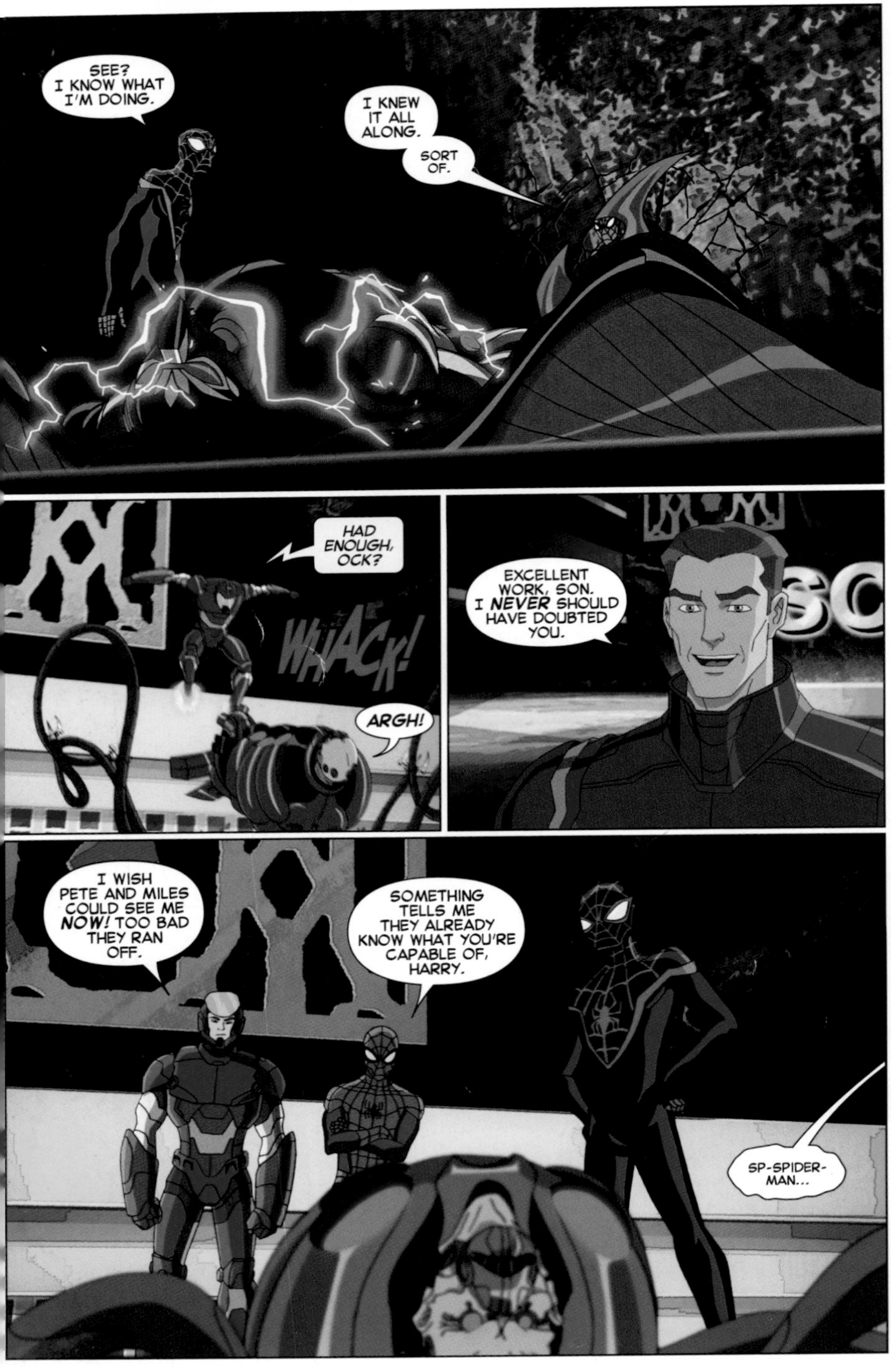
SEE? I KNOW WHAT I'M DOING.
I KNEW IT ALL ALONG.
SORT OF.
HAD ENOUGH, OCK?
WHACK!
ARGH!
EXCELLENT WORK, SON. I **NEVER** SHOULD HAVE DOUBTED YOU.
I WISH PETE AND MILES COULD SEE ME **NOW!** TOO BAD THEY RAN OFF.
SOMETHING TELLS ME THEY ALREADY KNOW WHAT YOU'RE CAPABLE OF, HARRY.
SP-SPIDER-MAN...

"...EVEN WITH DOCTOR OCTOPUS IN CUSTODY."

THE TRISKELION, S.H.I.E.L.D.'S BASE OF OPERATIONS.

THIS IS BUT A *TEMPORARY SETBACK* FOR MY *GENIUS.*

DO YOU REMEMBER THE *LAST* TIME YOU TRIED TO CONTAIN ME?

SURE. YOU BUSTED THE PLACE UP.

BUT THIS CELL IS BETTER. STRONGER. FACE IT, DOC--

"--YOU'RE STUCK HERE WITH US!"

LISTEN, MILES--I KNOW I'VE BEEN--

OVER-PROTECTIVE? PATRONIZING? I COULD KEEP GOING.

I WAS GOING FOR "ACTING LIKE A BIG BROTHER," BUT I GET THE POINT.

I MIGHT NOT BE AS *EXPERIENCED* A HERO AS YOU ARE, BUT I CAN PROVE THAT I'M *GOOD* AT IT IF YOU'D GIVE ME A CHANCE!

I *KNOW* YOU'RE *GREAT* AT BEING A HERO, IT'S JUST...IT WAS *MY* IDEA TO BRING YOU HERE FROM YOUR WORLD, AND NOW YOU'RE STRANDED ON MINE, AWAY FROM FAMILY AND FRIENDS, I--

I'M JUST TRYING TO GET YOU BACK HOME IN *ONE* PIECE.

MY BEING HERE ISN'T *YOUR* FAULT. I CAME HERE BY CHOICE. I WAS *EAGER* TO JOIN YOU BECAUSE I WANTED TO DO *GOOD.*

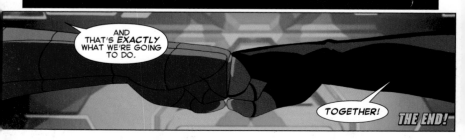

AND THAT'S *EXACTLY* WHAT WE'RE GOING TO DO.

TOGETHER!

THE END!

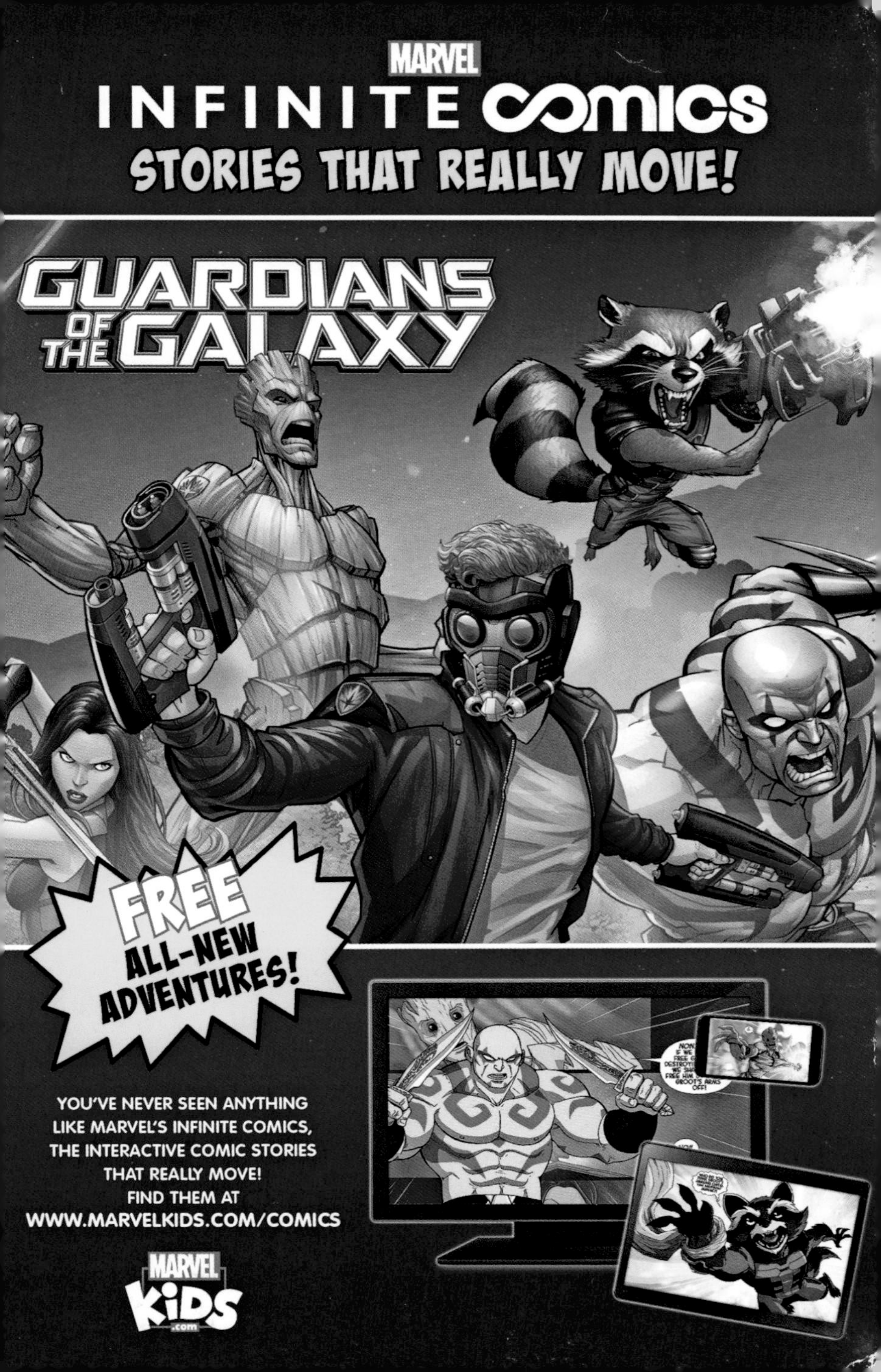

MARVEL
INFINITE COMICS
STORIES THAT REALLY MOVE!
GUARDIANS OF THE GALAXY
FREE
ALL-NEW ADVENTURES!
YOU'VE NEVER SEEN ANYTHING
LIKE MARVEL'S INFINITE COMICS,
THE INTERACTIVE COMIC STORIES
THAT REALLY MOVE!
FIND THEM AT
WWW.MARVELKIDS.COM/COMICS
MARVEL KIDS .com